The Bible: A Very Short Introduction

VERY SHORT INTRODUCTIONS are for anyone wanting a stimulating and accessible way into a new subject. They are written by experts, and have been translated into more than 45 different languages.

The series began in 1995, and now covers a wide variety of topics in every discipline. The VSI library currently contains over 650 volumes—a Very Short Introduction to everything from Psychology and Philosophy of Science to American History and Relativity—and continues to grow in every subject area.

Very Short Introductions available now:

ABOLITIONISM Richard S. Newman
THE ABRAHAMIC RELIGIONS Charles L. Cohen
ACCOUNTING Christopher Nobes
ADOLESCENCE Peter K. Smith
ADVERTISING Winston Fletcher
AERIAL WARFARE Frank Ledwidge
AESTHETICS Bence Nanay
AFRICAN AMERICAN RELIGION Eddie S. Glaude Jr
AFRICAN HISTORY John Parker and Richard Rathbone
AFRICAN POLITICS Ian Taylor
AFRICAN RELIGIONS Jacob K. Olupona
AGEING Nancy A. Pachana
AGNOSTICISM Robin Le Poidevin
AGRICULTURE Paul Brassley and Richard Soffe
ALEXANDER THE GREAT Hugh Bowden
ALGEBRA Peter M. Higgins
AMERICAN BUSINESS HISTORY Walter A. Friedman
AMERICAN CULTURAL HISTORY Eric Avila
AMERICAN FOREIGN RELATIONS Andrew Preston
AMERICAN HISTORY Paul S. Boyer
AMERICAN IMMIGRATION David A. Gerber
AMERICAN INTELLECTUAL HISTORY Jennifer Ratner-Rosenhagen
AMERICAN LEGAL HISTORY G. Edward White
AMERICAN MILITARY HISTORY Joseph T. Glatthaar
AMERICAN NAVAL HISTORY Craig L. Symonds
AMERICAN POLITICAL HISTORY Donald Critchlow
AMERICAN POLITICAL PARTIES AND ELECTIONS L. Sandy Maisel
AMERICAN POLITICS Richard M. Valelly
THE AMERICAN PRESIDENCY Charles O. Jones
THE AMERICAN REVOLUTION Robert J. Allison
AMERICAN SLAVERY Heather Andrea Williams
THE AMERICAN SOUTH Charles Reagan Wilson
THE AMERICAN WEST Stephen Aron
AMERICAN WOMEN'S HISTORY Susan Ware
AMPHIBIANS T. S. Kemp
ANAESTHESIA Aidan O'Donnell
ANALYTIC PHILOSOPHY Michael Beaney
ANARCHISM Colin Ward
ANCIENT ASSYRIA Karen Radner
ANCIENT EGYPT Ian Shaw
ANCIENT EGYPTIAN ART AND ARCHITECTURE Christina Riggs
ANCIENT GREECE Paul Cartledge

THE ANCIENT NEAR EAST
Amanda H. Podany
ANCIENT PHILOSOPHY Julia Annas
ANCIENT WARFARE Harry Sidebottom
ANGELS David Albert Jones
ANGLICANISM Mark Chapman
THE ANGLO-SAXON AGE John Blair
ANIMAL BEHAVIOUR
Tristram D. Wyatt
THE ANIMAL KINGDOM
Peter Holland
ANIMAL RIGHTS David DeGrazia
THE ANTARCTIC Klaus Dodds
ANTHROPOCENE Erle C. Ellis
ANTISEMITISM Steven Beller
ANXIETY Daniel Freeman and
Jason Freeman
THE APOCRYPHAL GOSPELS
Paul Foster
APPLIED MATHEMATICS
Alain Goriely
THOMAS AQUINAS Fergus Kerr
ARBITRATION Thomas Schultz and
Thomas Grant
ARCHAEOLOGY Paul Bahn
ARCHITECTURE Andrew Ballantyne
ARISTOCRACY William Doyle
ARISTOTLE Jonathan Barnes
ART HISTORY Dana Arnold
ART THEORY Cynthia Freeland
ARTIFICIAL INTELLIGENCE
Margaret A. Boden
ASIAN AMERICAN HISTORY
Madeline Y. Hsu
ASTROBIOLOGY David C. Catling
ASTROPHYSICS James Binney
ATHEISM Julian Baggini
THE ATMOSPHERE Paul I. Palmer
AUGUSTINE Henry Chadwick
AUSTRALIA Kenneth Morgan
AUTISM Uta Frith
AUTOBIOGRAPHY Laura Marcus
THE AVANT GARDE David Cottington
THE AZTECS Davíd Carrasco
BABYLONIA Trevor Bryce
BACTERIA Sebastian G. B. Amyes
BANKING John Goddard and
John O. S. Wilson
BARTHES Jonathan Culler
THE BEATS David Sterritt
BEAUTY Roger Scruton
BEHAVIOURAL ECONOMICS
Michelle Baddeley
BESTSELLERS John Sutherland
THE BIBLE John Riches
BIBLICAL ARCHAEOLOGY
Eric H. Cline
BIG DATA Dawn E. Holmes
BIOCHEMISTRY Mark Lorch
BIOGEOGRAPHY Mark V. Lomolino
BIOGRAPHY Hermione Lee
BIOMETRICS Michael Fairhurst
BLACK HOLES Katherine Blundell
BLASPHEMY Yvonne Sherwood
BLOOD Chris Cooper
THE BLUES Elijah Wald
THE BODY Chris Shilling
THE BOOK OF COMMON PRAYER
Brian Cummings
THE BOOK OF MORMON
Terryl Givens
BORDERS Alexander C. Diener and
Joshua Hagen
THE BRAIN Michael O'Shea
BRANDING Robert Jones
THE BRICS Andrew F. Cooper
THE BRITISH CONSTITUTION
Martin Loughlin
THE BRITISH EMPIRE Ashley Jackson
BRITISH POLITICS Tony Wright
BUDDHA Michael Carrithers
BUDDHISM Damien Keown
BUDDHIST ETHICS Damien Keown
BYZANTIUM Peter Sarris
CALVINISM Jon Balserak
ALBERT CAMUS Oliver Gloag
CANADA Donald Wright
CANCER Nicholas James
CAPITALISM James Fulcher
CATHOLICISM Gerald O'Collins
CAUSATION Stephen Mumford and
Rani Lill Anjum
THE CELL Terence Allen and
Graham Cowling
THE CELTS Barry Cunliffe
CHAOS Leonard Smith
GEOFFREY CHAUCER David Wallace
CHEMISTRY Peter Atkins
CHILD PSYCHOLOGY
Usha Goswami

CHILDREN'S LITERATURE Kimberley Reynolds
CHINESE LITERATURE Sabina Knight
CHOICE THEORY Michael Allingham
CHRISTIAN ART Beth Williamson
CHRISTIAN ETHICS D. Stephen Long
CHRISTIANITY Linda Woodhead
CIRCADIAN RHYTHMS Russell Foster and Leon Kreitzman
CITIZENSHIP Richard Bellamy
CITY PLANNING Carl Abbott
CIVIL ENGINEERING David Muir Wood
CLASSICAL LITERATURE William Allan
CLASSICAL MYTHOLOGY Helen Morales
CLASSICS Mary Beard and John Henderson
CLAUSEWITZ Michael Howard
CLIMATE Mark Maslin
CLIMATE CHANGE Mark Maslin
CLINICAL PSYCHOLOGY Susan Llewelyn and Katie Aafjes-van Doorn
COGNITIVE NEUROSCIENCE Richard Passingham
THE COLD WAR Robert J. McMahon
COLONIAL AMERICA Alan Taylor
COLONIAL LATIN AMERICAN LITERATURE Rolena Adorno
COMBINATORICS Robin Wilson
COMEDY Matthew Bevis
COMMUNISM Leslie Holmes
COMPARATIVE LITERATURE Ben Hutchinson
COMPETITION AND ANTITRUST LAW Ariel Ezrachi
COMPLEXITY John H. Holland
THE COMPUTER Darrel Ince
COMPUTER SCIENCE Subrata Dasgupta
CONCENTRATION CAMPS Dan Stone
CONFUCIANISM Daniel K. Gardner
THE CONQUISTADORS Matthew Restall and Felipe Fernández-Armesto
CONSCIENCE Paul Strohm
CONSCIOUSNESS Susan Blackmore
CONTEMPORARY ART Julian Stallabrass
CONTEMPORARY FICTION Robert Eaglestone
CONTINENTAL PHILOSOPHY Simon Critchley
COPERNICUS Owen Gingerich
CORAL REEFS Charles Sheppard
CORPORATE SOCIAL RESPONSIBILITY Jeremy Moon
CORRUPTION Leslie Holmes
COSMOLOGY Peter Coles
COUNTRY MUSIC Richard Carlin
CREATIVITY Vlad Glăveanu
CRIME FICTION Richard Bradford
CRIMINAL JUSTICE Julian V. Roberts
CRIMINOLOGY Tim Newburn
CRITICAL THEORY Stephen Eric Bronner
THE CRUSADES Christopher Tyerman
CRYPTOGRAPHY Fred Piper and Sean Murphy
CRYSTALLOGRAPHY A. M. Glazer
THE CULTURAL REVOLUTION Richard Curt Kraus
DADA AND SURREALISM David Hopkins
DANTE Peter Hainsworth and David Robey
DARWIN Jonathan Howard
THE DEAD SEA SCROLLS Timothy H. Lim
DECADENCE David Weir
DECOLONIZATION Dane Kennedy
DEMENTIA Kathleen Taylor
DEMOCRACY Bernard Crick
DEMOGRAPHY Sarah Harper
DEPRESSION Jan Scott and Mary Jane Tacchi
DERRIDA Simon Glendinning
DESCARTES Tom Sorell
DESERTS Nick Middleton
DESIGN John Heskett
DEVELOPMENT Ian Goldin
DEVELOPMENTAL BIOLOGY Lewis Wolpert
THE DEVIL Darren Oldridge
DIASPORA Kevin Kenny
CHARLES DICKENS Jenny Hartley
DICTIONARIES Lynda Mugglestone
DINOSAURS David Norman

DIPLOMATIC HISTORY
Joseph M. Siracusa
DOCUMENTARY FILM
Patricia Aufderheide
DREAMING J. Allan Hobson
DRUGS Les Iversen
DRUIDS Barry Cunliffe
DYNASTY Jeroen Duindam
DYSLEXIA Margaret J. Snowling
EARLY MUSIC Thomas Forrest Kelly
THE EARTH Martin Redfern
EARTH SYSTEM SCIENCE Tim Lenton
ECOLOGY Jaboury Ghazoul
ECONOMICS Partha Dasgupta
EDUCATION Gary Thomas
EGYPTIAN MYTH Geraldine Pinch
EIGHTEENTH-CENTURY BRITAIN
Paul Langford
THE ELEMENTS Philip Ball
EMOTION Dylan Evans
EMPIRE Stephen Howe
ENERGY SYSTEMS Nick Jenkins
ENGELS Terrell Carver
ENGINEERING David Blockley
THE ENGLISH LANGUAGE
Simon Horobin
ENGLISH LITERATURE Jonathan Bate
THE ENLIGHTENMENT
John Robertson
ENTREPRENEURSHIP Paul Westhead
and Mike Wright
ENVIRONMENTAL ECONOMICS
Stephen Smith
ENVIRONMENTAL ETHICS
Robin Attfield
ENVIRONMENTAL LAW
Elizabeth Fisher
ENVIRONMENTAL POLITICS
Andrew Dobson
ENZYMES Paul Engel
EPICUREANISM Catherine Wilson
EPIDEMIOLOGY Rodolfo Saracci
ETHICS Simon Blackburn
ETHNOMUSICOLOGY Timothy Rice
THE ETRUSCANS Christopher Smith
EUGENICS Philippa Levine
THE EUROPEAN UNION
Simon Usherwood and John Pinder
EUROPEAN UNION LAW
Anthony Arnull
EVOLUTION Brian and
Deborah Charlesworth
EXISTENTIALISM Thomas Flynn
EXPLORATION Stewart A. Weaver
EXTINCTION Paul B. Wignall
THE EYE Michael Land
FAIRY TALE Marina Warner
FAMILY LAW Jonathan Herring
MICHAEL FARADAY
Frank A. J. L. James
FASCISM Kevin Passmore
FASHION Rebecca Arnold
FEDERALISM Mark J. Rozell and
Clyde Wilcox
FEMINISM Margaret Walters
FILM Michael Wood
FILM MUSIC Kathryn Kalinak
FILM NOIR James Naremore
FIRE Andrew C. Scott
THE FIRST WORLD WAR
Michael Howard
FOLK MUSIC Mark Slobin
FOOD John Krebs
FORENSIC PSYCHOLOGY
David Canter
FORENSIC SCIENCE Jim Fraser
FORESTS Jaboury Ghazoul
FOSSILS Keith Thomson
FOUCAULT Gary Gutting
THE FOUNDING FATHERS
R. B. Bernstein
FRACTALS Kenneth Falconer
FREE SPEECH Nigel Warburton
FREE WILL Thomas Pink
FREEMASONRY Andreas Önnerfors
FRENCH LITERATURE John D. Lyons
FRENCH PHILOSOPHY
Stephen Gaukroger and Knox Peden
THE FRENCH REVOLUTION
William Doyle
FREUD Anthony Storr
FUNDAMENTALISM Malise Ruthven
FUNGI Nicholas P. Money
THE FUTURE Jennifer M. Gidley
GALAXIES John Gribbin
GALILEO Stillman Drake
GAME THEORY Ken Binmore
GANDHI Bhikhu Parekh
GARDEN HISTORY Gordon Campbell
GENES Jonathan Slack

GENIUS Andrew Robinson
GENOMICS John Archibald
GEOGRAPHY John Matthews and David Herbert
GEOLOGY Jan Zalasiewicz
GEOPHYSICS William Lowrie
GEOPOLITICS Klaus Dodds
GERMAN LITERATURE Nicholas Boyle
GERMAN PHILOSOPHY Andrew Bowie
THE GHETTO Bryan Cheyette
GLACIATION David J. A. Evans
GLOBAL CATASTROPHES Bill McGuire
GLOBAL ECONOMIC HISTORY Robert C. Allen
GLOBAL ISLAM Nile Green
GLOBALIZATION Manfred B. Steger
GOD John Bowker
GOETHE Ritchie Robertson
THE GOTHIC Nick Groom
GOVERNANCE Mark Bevir
GRAVITY Timothy Clifton
THE GREAT DEPRESSION AND THE NEW DEAL Eric Rauchway
HABEAS CORPUS Amanda Tyler
HABERMAS James Gordon Finlayson
THE HABSBURG EMPIRE Martyn Rady
HAPPINESS Daniel M. Haybron
THE HARLEM RENAISSANCE Cheryl A. Wall
THE HEBREW BIBLE AS LITERATURE Tod Linafelt
HEGEL Peter Singer
HEIDEGGER Michael Inwood
THE HELLENISTIC AGE Peter Thonemann
HEREDITY John Waller
HERMENEUTICS Jens Zimmermann
HERODOTUS Jennifer T. Roberts
HIEROGLYPHS Penelope Wilson
HINDUISM Kim Knott
HISTORY John H. Arnold
THE HISTORY OF ASTRONOMY Michael Hoskin
THE HISTORY OF CHEMISTRY William H. Brock
THE HISTORY OF CHILDHOOD James Marten
THE HISTORY OF CINEMA Geoffrey Nowell-Smith
THE HISTORY OF LIFE Michael Benton
THE HISTORY OF MATHEMATICS Jacqueline Stedall
THE HISTORY OF MEDICINE William Bynum
THE HISTORY OF PHYSICS J. L. Heilbron
THE HISTORY OF TIME Leofranc Holford-Strevens
HIV AND AIDS Alan Whiteside
HOBBES Richard Tuck
HOLLYWOOD Peter Decherney
THE HOLY ROMAN EMPIRE Joachim Whaley
HOME Michael Allen Fox
HOMER Barbara Graziosi
HORMONES Martin Luck
HORROR Darryl Jones
HUMAN ANATOMY Leslie Klenerman
HUMAN EVOLUTION Bernard Wood
HUMAN PHYSIOLOGY Jamie A. Davies
HUMAN RIGHTS Andrew Clapham
HUMANISM Stephen Law
HUME James A. Harris
HUMOUR Noël Carroll
THE ICE AGE Jamie Woodward
IDENTITY Florian Coulmas
IDEOLOGY Michael Freeden
THE IMMUNE SYSTEM Paul Klenerman
INDIAN CINEMA Ashish Rajadhyaksha
INDIAN PHILOSOPHY Sue Hamilton
THE INDUSTRIAL REVOLUTION Robert C. Allen
INFECTIOUS DISEASE Marta L. Wayne and Benjamin M. Bolker
INFINITY Ian Stewart
INFORMATION Luciano Floridi
INNOVATION Mark Dodgson and David Gann
INTELLECTUAL PROPERTY Siva Vaidhyanathan
INTELLIGENCE Ian J. Deary

INTERNATIONAL LAW Vaughan Lowe
INTERNATIONAL MIGRATION Khalid Koser
INTERNATIONAL RELATIONS Christian Reus-Smit
INTERNATIONAL SECURITY Christopher S. Browning
IRAN Ali M. Ansari
ISLAM Malise Ruthven
ISLAMIC HISTORY Adam Silverstein
ISLAMIC LAW Mashood A. Baderin
ISOTOPES Rob Ellam
ITALIAN LITERATURE Peter Hainsworth and David Robey
HENRY JAMES Susan L. Mizruchi
JESUS Richard Bauckham
JEWISH HISTORY David N. Myers
JEWISH LITERATURE Ilan Stavans
JOURNALISM Ian Hargreaves
JAMES JOYCE Colin MacCabe
JUDAISM Norman Solomon
JUNG Anthony Stevens
KABBALAH Joseph Dan
KAFKA Ritchie Robertson
KANT Roger Scruton
KEYNES Robert Skidelsky
KIERKEGAARD Patrick Gardiner
KNOWLEDGE Jennifer Nagel
THE KORAN Michael Cook
KOREA Michael J. Seth
LAKES Warwick F. Vincent
LANDSCAPE ARCHITECTURE Ian H. Thompson
LANDSCAPES AND GEOMORPHOLOGY Andrew Goudie and Heather Viles
LANGUAGES Stephen R. Anderson
LATE ANTIQUITY Gillian Clark
LAW Raymond Wacks
THE LAWS OF THERMODYNAMICS Peter Atkins
LEADERSHIP Keith Grint
LEARNING Mark Haselgrove
LEIBNIZ Maria Rosa Antognazza
C. S. LEWIS James Como
LIBERALISM Michael Freeden
LIGHT Ian Walmsley
LINCOLN Allen C. Guelzo
LINGUISTICS Peter Matthews
LITERARY THEORY Jonathan Culler
LOCKE John Dunn
LOGIC Graham Priest
LOVE Ronald de Sousa
MARTIN LUTHER Scott H. Hendrix
MACHIAVELLI Quentin Skinner
MADNESS Andrew Scull
MAGIC Owen Davies
MAGNA CARTA Nicholas Vincent
MAGNETISM Stephen Blundell
MALTHUS Donald Winch
MAMMALS T. S. Kemp
MANAGEMENT John Hendry
NELSON MANDELA Elleke Boehmer
MAO Delia Davin
MARINE BIOLOGY Philip V. Mladenov
MARKETING Kenneth Le Meunier-FitzHugh
THE MARQUIS DE SADE John Phillips
MARTYRDOM Jolyon Mitchell
MARX Peter Singer
MATERIALS Christopher Hall
MATHEMATICAL FINANCE Mark H. A. Davis
MATHEMATICS Timothy Gowers
MATTER Geoff Cottrell
THE MAYA Matthew Restall and Amara Solari
THE MEANING OF LIFE Terry Eagleton
MEASUREMENT David Hand
MEDICAL ETHICS Michael Dunn and Tony Hope
MEDICAL LAW Charles Foster
MEDIEVAL BRITAIN John Gillingham and Ralph A. Griffiths
MEDIEVAL LITERATURE Elaine Treharne
MEDIEVAL PHILOSOPHY John Marenbon
MEMORY Jonathan K. Foster
METAPHYSICS Stephen Mumford
METHODISM William J. Abraham
THE MEXICAN REVOLUTION Alan Knight
MICROBIOLOGY Nicholas P. Money
MICROECONOMICS Avinash Dixit
MICROSCOPY Terence Allen
THE MIDDLE AGES Miri Rubin

MILITARY JUSTICE Eugene R. Fidell
MILITARY STRATEGY
Antulio J. Echevarria II
MINERALS David Vaughan
MIRACLES Yujin Nagasawa
MODERN ARCHITECTURE
Adam Sharr
MODERN ART David Cottington
MODERN BRAZIL Anthony W. Pereira
MODERN CHINA Rana Mitter
MODERN DRAMA
Kirsten E. Shepherd-Barr
MODERN FRANCE
Vanessa R. Schwartz
MODERN INDIA Craig Jeffrey
MODERN IRELAND Senia Pašeta
MODERN ITALY Anna Cento Bull
MODERN JAPAN
Christopher Goto-Jones
MODERN LATIN AMERICAN LITERATURE
Roberto González Echevarría
MODERN WAR Richard English
MODERNISM Christopher Butler
MOLECULAR BIOLOGY Aysha Divan and Janice A. Royds
MOLECULES Philip Ball
MONASTICISM Stephen J. Davis
THE MONGOLS Morris Rossabi
MONTAIGNE William M. Hamlin
MOONS David A. Rothery
MORMONISM Richard Lyman Bushman
MOUNTAINS Martin F. Price
MUHAMMAD Jonathan A. C. Brown
MULTICULTURALISM Ali Rattansi
MULTILINGUALISM John C. Maher
MUSIC Nicholas Cook
MYTH Robert A. Segal
NAPOLEON David Bell
THE NAPOLEONIC WARS
Mike Rapport
NATIONALISM Steven Grosby
NATIVE AMERICAN LITERATURE
Sean Teuton
NAVIGATION Jim Bennett
NAZI GERMANY Jane Caplan
NEOLIBERALISM Manfred B. Steger and Ravi K. Roy
NETWORKS Guido Caldarelli and Michele Catanzaro
THE NEW TESTAMENT
LUKE TIMOTHY JOHNSON
THE NEW TESTAMENT AS LITERATURE Kyle Keefer
NEWTON Robert Iliffe
NIELS BOHR J. L. Heilbron
NIETZSCHE Michael Tanner
NINETEENTH-CENTURY BRITAIN Christopher Harvie and H. C. G. Matthew
THE NORMAN CONQUEST
George Garnett
NORTH AMERICAN INDIANS
Theda Perdue and Michael D. Green
NORTHERN IRELAND
Marc Mulholland
NOTHING Frank Close
NUCLEAR PHYSICS Frank Close
NUCLEAR POWER Maxwell Irvine
NUCLEAR WEAPONS
Joseph M. Siracusa
NUMBER THEORY Robin Wilson
NUMBERS Peter M. Higgins
NUTRITION David A. Bender
OBJECTIVITY Stephen Gaukroger
OCEANS Dorrik Stow
THE OLD TESTAMENT
Michael D. Coogan
THE ORCHESTRA D. Kern Holoman
ORGANIC CHEMISTRY
Graham Patrick
ORGANIZATIONS Mary Jo Hatch
ORGANIZED CRIME
Georgios A. Antonopoulos and Georgios Papanicolaou
ORTHODOX CHRISTIANITY
A. Edward Siecienski
OVID Llewelyn Morgan
PAGANISM Owen Davies
THE PALESTINIAN-ISRAELI CONFLICT Martin Bunton
PANDEMICS Christian W. McMillen
PARTICLE PHYSICS Frank Close
PAUL E. P. Sanders
PEACE Oliver P. Richmond
PENTECOSTALISM William K. Kay
PERCEPTION Brian Rogers
THE PERIODIC TABLE Eric R. Scerri
PHILOSOPHICAL METHOD
Timothy Williamson

PHILOSOPHY Edward Craig
PHILOSOPHY IN THE ISLAMIC WORLD Peter Adamson
PHILOSOPHY OF BIOLOGY Samir Okasha
PHILOSOPHY OF LAW Raymond Wacks
PHILOSOPHY OF PHYSICS David Wallace
PHILOSOPHY OF SCIENCE Samir Okasha
PHILOSOPHY OF RELIGION Tim Bayne
PHOTOGRAPHY Steve Edwards
PHYSICAL CHEMISTRY Peter Atkins
PHYSICS Sidney Perkowitz
PILGRIMAGE Ian Reader
PLAGUE Paul Slack
PLANETS David A. Rothery
PLANTS Timothy Walker
PLATE TECTONICS Peter Molnar
PLATO Julia Annas
POETRY Bernard O'Donoghue
POLITICAL PHILOSOPHY David Miller
POLITICS Kenneth Minogue
POPULISM Cas Mudde and Cristóbal Rovira Kaltwasser
POSTCOLONIALISM Robert Young
POSTMODERNISM Christopher Butler
POSTSTRUCTURALISM Catherine Belsey
POVERTY Philip N. Jefferson
PREHISTORY Chris Gosden
PRESOCRATIC PHILOSOPHY Catherine Osborne
PRIVACY Raymond Wacks
PROBABILITY John Haigh
PROGRESSIVISM Walter Nugent
PROHIBITION W. J. Rorabaugh
PROJECTS Andrew Davies
PROTESTANTISM Mark A. Noll
PSYCHIATRY Tom Burns
PSYCHOANALYSIS Daniel Pick
PSYCHOLOGY Gillian Butler and Freda McManus
PSYCHOLOGY OF MUSIC Elizabeth Hellmuth Margulis
PSYCHOPATHY Essi Viding
PSYCHOTHERAPY Tom Burns and Eva Burns-Lundgren
PUBLIC ADMINISTRATION Stella Z. Theodoulou and Ravi K. Roy
PUBLIC HEALTH Virginia Berridge
PURITANISM Francis J. Bremer
THE QUAKERS Pink Dandelion
QUANTUM THEORY John Polkinghorne
RACISM Ali Rattansi
RADIOACTIVITY Claudio Tuniz
RASTAFARI Ennis B. Edmonds
READING Belinda Jack
THE REAGAN REVOLUTION Gil Troy
REALITY Jan Westerhoff
RECONSTRUCTION Allen C. Guelzo
THE REFORMATION Peter Marshall
REFUGEES Gil Loescher
RELATIVITY Russell Stannard
RELIGION Thomas A. Tweed
RELIGION IN AMERICA Timothy Beal
THE RENAISSANCE Jerry Brotton
RENAISSANCE ART Geraldine A. Johnson
RENEWABLE ENERGY Nick Jelley
REPTILES T. S. Kemp
REVOLUTIONS Jack A. Goldstone
RHETORIC Richard Toye
RISK Baruch Fischhoff and John Kadvany
RITUAL Barry Stephenson
RIVERS Nick Middleton
ROBOTICS Alan Winfield
ROCKS Jan Zalasiewicz
ROMAN BRITAIN Peter Salway
THE ROMAN EMPIRE Christopher Kelly
THE ROMAN REPUBLIC David M. Gwynn
ROMANTICISM Michael Ferber
ROUSSEAU Robert Wokler
RUSSELL A. C. Grayling
THE RUSSIAN ECONOMY Richard Connolly
RUSSIAN HISTORY Geoffrey Hosking
RUSSIAN LITERATURE Catriona Kelly
THE RUSSIAN REVOLUTION S. A. Smith
SAINTS Simon Yarrow
SAMURAI Michael Wert
SAVANNAS Peter A. Furley

SCEPTICISM Duncan Pritchard
SCHIZOPHRENIA Chris Frith and Eve Johnstone
SCHOPENHAUER Christopher Janaway
SCIENCE AND RELIGION Thomas Dixon
SCIENCE FICTION David Seed
THE SCIENTIFIC REVOLUTION Lawrence M. Principe
SCOTLAND Rab Houston
SECULARISM Andrew Copson
SEXUAL SELECTION Marlene Zuk and Leigh W. Simmons
SEXUALITY Véronique Mottier
WILLIAM SHAKESPEARE Stanley Wells
SHAKESPEARE'S COMEDIES Bart van Es
SHAKESPEARE'S SONNETS AND POEMS Jonathan F. S. Post
SHAKESPEARE'S TRAGEDIES Stanley Wells
GEORGE BERNARD SHAW Christopher Wixson
SIKHISM Eleanor Nesbitt
SILENT FILM Donna Kornhaber
THE SILK ROAD James A. Millward
SLANG Jonathon Green
SLEEP Steven W. Lockley and Russell G. Foster
SMELL Matthew Cobb
ADAM SMITH Christopher J. Berry
SOCIAL AND CULTURAL ANTHROPOLOGY John Monaghan and Peter Just
SOCIAL PSYCHOLOGY Richard J. Crisp
SOCIAL WORK Sally Holland and Jonathan Scourfield
SOCIALISM Michael Newman
SOCIOLINGUISTICS John Edwards
SOCIOLOGY Steve Bruce
SOCRATES C. C. W. Taylor
SOFT MATTER Tom McLeish
SOUND Mike Goldsmith
SOUTHEAST ASIA James R. Rush
THE SOVIET UNION Stephen Lovell
THE SPANISH CIVIL WAR Helen Graham
SPANISH LITERATURE Jo Labanyi
SPINOZA Roger Scruton
SPIRITUALITY Philip Sheldrake
SPORT Mike Cronin
STARS Andrew King
STATISTICS David J. Hand
STEM CELLS Jonathan Slack
STOICISM Brad Inwood
STRUCTURAL ENGINEERING David Blockley
STUART BRITAIN John Morrill
THE SUN Philip Judge
SUPERCONDUCTIVITY Stephen Blundell
SUPERSTITION Stuart Vyse
SYMMETRY Ian Stewart
SYNAESTHESIA Julia Simner
SYNTHETIC BIOLOGY Jamie A. Davies
SYSTEMS BIOLOGY Eberhard O. Voit
TAXATION Stephen Smith
TEETH Peter S. Ungar
TELESCOPES Geoff Cottrell
TERRORISM Charles Townshend
THEATRE Marvin Carlson
THEOLOGY David F. Ford
THINKING AND REASONING Jonathan St B. T. Evans
THOUGHT Tim Bayne
TIBETAN BUDDHISM Matthew T. Kapstein
TIDES David George Bowers and Emyr Martyn Roberts
TIME Jenann Ismael
TOCQUEVILLE Harvey C. Mansfield
LEO TOLSTOY Liza Knapp
TOPOLOGY Richard Earl
TRAGEDY Adrian Poole
TRANSLATION Matthew Reynolds
THE TREATY OF VERSAILLES Michael S. Neiberg
TRIGONOMETRY Glen Van Brummelen
THE TROJAN WAR Eric H. Cline
TRUST Katherine Hawley
THE TUDORS John Guy
TWENTIETH-CENTURY BRITAIN Kenneth O. Morgan
TYPOGRAPHY Paul Luna
THE UNITED NATIONS Jussi M. Hanhimäki

UNIVERSITIES AND COLLEGES David Palfreyman and Paul Temple
THE U.S. CIVIL WAR Louis P. Masur
THE U.S. CONGRESS Donald A. Ritchie
THE U.S. CONSTITUTION David J. Bodenhamer
THE U.S. SUPREME COURT Linda Greenhouse
UTILITARIANISM Katarzyna de Lazari-Radek and Peter Singer
UTOPIANISM Lyman Tower Sargent
VETERINARY SCIENCE James Yeates
THE VIKINGS Julian D. Richards
THE VIRGIN MARY Mary Joan Winn Leith
THE VIRTUES Craig A. Boyd and Kevin Timpe
VIRUSES Dorothy H. Crawford
VOLCANOES Michael J. Branney and Jan Zalasiewicz
VOLTAIRE Nicholas Cronk
WAR AND RELIGION Jolyon Mitchell and Joshua Rey
WAR AND TECHNOLOGY Alex Roland
WATER John Finney
WAVES Mike Goldsmith
WEATHER Storm Dunlop
THE WELFARE STATE David Garland
WITCHCRAFT Malcolm Gaskill
WITTGENSTEIN A. C. Grayling
WORK Stephen Fineman
WORLD MUSIC Philip Bohlman
THE WORLD TRADE ORGANIZATION Amrita Narlikar
WORLD WAR II Gerhard L. Weinberg
WRITING AND SCRIPT Andrew Robinson
ZIONISM Michael Stanislawski
ÉMILE ZOLA Brian Nelson

Available soon:

PHILOSOPHY OF MIND Barbara Gail Montero
PLANETARY SYSTEMS Raymond T. Pierrehumbert
PAKISTAN Pippa Virdee
THE ARCTIC Klaus Dodds and Jamie Woodward
THE HISTORY OF POLITICAL THOUGHT Richard Whatmore

For more information visit our website

www.oup.com/vsi/

John Riches

THE BIBLE

A Very Short Introduction

SECOND EDITION

OXFORD
UNIVERSITY PRESS

Great Clarendon Street, Oxford, OX2 6DP,
United Kingdom

Oxford University Press is a department of the University of Oxford. It furthers the University's objective of excellence in research, scholarship, and education by publishing worldwide. Oxford is a registered trade mark of Oxford University Press in the UK and in certain other countries

First edition published 2000
This edition published 2021

Published in the United States of America by Oxford University Press
198 Madison Avenue, New York, NY 10016, United States of America

British Library Cataloguing in Publication Data
Data available

Library of Congress Control Number: 2021938334

ISBN 978-0-19-886333-5

Printed and bound by
CPI Group (UK) Ltd, Croydon, CR0 4YY

Contents

List of illustrations

Chapter 1
The Bible in the modern world: classic or sacred text?

It is sometimes said that there are more unread copies of the Bible than of any other book in the world. Such a claim is difficult to prove, though it clearly reflects widespread concern among Christians in Europe about growing levels of ignorance of the Bible's contents. However, it also misses an arguably more significant truth, namely that the Bible is still one of the most influential and widely read books in the world.

It would be interesting to run a competition to find out Today's Most Influential Book and Today's Most Read Book in the World—not by any means the same thing. Marx's *Das Kapital* might until recently have qualified for the first, though hardly for the second; Thomas Paine's *The Rights of Man* and Adam Smith's *The Wealth of Nations* might get shortlisted for the first too. There would surely be candidates of this kind from the sciences (such as Darwin's *Origin of Species*), and from philosophy, literature, and the arts. How would they fare in relation to the great central texts of the major world faiths? 'Influence' is not too precise a measure and the eventual outcome of such a competition would probably say as much about the judges as about the winner.

Contemporary lists of Most Read Books in the World agree that the Bible outstrips all other books, with estimates of some 2.5 billion sales and a far larger number of copies distributed free of charge. Other major religious texts also receive high listings: the Qur'ān: 800 million, *The Book of Mormon*: 150 million.

Other titles which have sold over 100 million copies include some literary classics, Dickens's *Tale of Two Cities*, Tolkien's *Lord of the Rings*, popular works of crime fiction such as Agatha Christie's *And Then There Were None*, and J. K. Rowling's Harry Potter books. Tying with the *Book of Mormon* and *The Lord of the Rings* is Baden-Powell's *Scouting for Boys*.

From time to time certain political texts may emerge to challenge the position of works such as the Qur'ān and the Bible at or near the top of both lists. Chairman Mao's Little Red Book in its day had a massive readership, 800–900 million, and was hugely influential. Its current influence is less clear. The major religious texts probably have the greater staying power.

The point of this imaginary competition is not to claim any particular moral or aesthetic superiority for any particular text. That would have to be argued on quite different grounds, if it could be argued at all. The point is to show up something of the very special quality of such major religious texts. They are immensely influential over people's lives and are read by people of vastly different educational and cultural backgrounds. How do they do it?

It is not my task to answer that question for the Qur'ān, interesting though it would be to consider what these two texts have in common. It is, however, the major purpose of this Very Short Introduction to answer it for the Bible. Why does this ancient collection of texts continue to exercise such power over people's lives in our modern, post-colonial, post-industrial world?

Let me first however introduce some of today's Bible readers, simply to communicate something of its extraordinary appeal, its ability to speak, negatively or positively, to people of different education, culture, and beliefs; but also to portray something of the great diversity of readings which spring from it.

Mary John Mananzan is a Benedictine sister from the Philippines, who is also chairperson of Gabriela, a women's organization with 40,000 members from grassroots organizations. This involvement in the struggle for women's dignity and rights led her to question the type of devotion to Mary which was prevalent. Filipina women are encouraged to be submissive and obedient to their husbands and superiors, as Mary was submissive to God's purposes in agreeing to bear his son: 'be it unto me according to thy word'. Mary John found ammunition against such kinds of Marian piety in Mary's hymn of praise in Luke's Gospel, known in the church as the Magnificat. In it she sings of her God:

> He has shown strength with his arm,
> he has scattered the proud in the thoughts of their hearts,
> he has brought down the powerful from their thrones,
> and lifted up the lowly;
> he has filled the hungry with good things,
> and sent the rich away empty.
>
> Luke 1:46–55

Here was a vision of a Mary altogether more active and subversive, who worships a God who supports the poor and dispossesses the wealthy. Mary John took the students in her classes on demonstrations. 'Teaching social action not social graces' was how an article in the *New York Herald Tribune* described it. Forty years later she is still being accused by Duterte's government of being a communist and a terrorist.

Bishop Dinis Sengulane is an Anglican bishop in Mozambique. After independence in 1975, the country was racked by a terrible civil war between RENAMO and FRELIMO. Bishop Dinis was part of a church group involved in the—ultimately remarkably successful—peace process. At one crucial meeting with the RENAMO leader, he took out his Bible and read two verses from the Sermon on the Mount (Matthew 5:7, 9):

> Blessed are the merciful, for they will receive mercy.
> Blessed are the peacemakers, for they will be called children of God.

He pleaded with the leader to have mercy on the people of Mozambique and to stop the fighting. He appealed to him to become a peacemaker, for then he would be called a son of God. 'If however you choose not to work for peace,' continued the bishop, 'then we shall want to know whose son you are.' The leader asked Bishop Dinis to leave his Bible behind so that he could use it with his generals.

Daniel Boyarin is Professor of Talmudic Culture at the University of California, Berkeley. In his book *A Radical Jew: Paul and the Politics of Identity*, he argues that Paul, precisely as a Jew, was profoundly critical of those tendencies in the tradition which emphasized Jewish difference and particularity. 'There is no longer Jew or Greek, there is no longer slave or free, there is no longer neither male and female; for all of you are one in Christ Jesus' (Galatians 3:28).

Such universalizing tendencies are not, however, without their dangers. What about those who wish to hold on to the old distinctions? What place is there for them in this brave new world? The subsequent history of Jewish–Christian relations shows how terrible the consequences of this refusal to recognize the particular identity of the Jews have been. But equally, Jewish desire to restore and maintain their particular attachments to the Land of Israel has brought its own severe problems. Paul's cultural critique of Judaism has to be heard, just as it too has to be subjected to radical critique. Boyarin's view is that Jewish existence in the Diaspora (that is to say, in Jewish communities outside Israel) is a better model for intercommunity relations than the Zionist vision of restoration. Boyarin holds dual US and Israeli citizenship.

Tracy Mitchell trained as a chemical engineer and started her career working for an international drinks company. From there she moved into fair trade finance and now is managing director of a small fair trade business in Paisley which imports food products from smallholder farmers in Africa and Asia. It's a business which brings her into close partnership with some very resourceful people living on the edge, which is full of unknown risks and unusual challenges. Her faith is based in close study and daily reading of the Bible. She writes:

> Whilst there are a number of bible verses that inspire my day to day life, Micah 6:8 is probably the most significant. Over the last 15 or so years I have devoted a large part of my daily life to fair trade related projects. My passion for fair trade comes from my faith in a generous God who has loved us in sending Jesus Christ, and calls us now to 'act justly, love mercy and walk humbly' as we love our neighbours.
>
> As I have faced challenges in my work I have often been taken about by how directly God speaks into the situation through His Word and my daily readings. Verses that have really struck me over the last couple of years have included Exodus 14:14 (the Lord will fight for you; you need only to be still), and Isaiah 43:2 (particularly the Message version 'when you are in over your head, I'll be there with you'). (personal communication)

One last example of a Bible reader less attractive to liberal sentiment. In his fascinating travel narrative *The Divine Supermarket*, Malise Ruthven describes a meeting with the Reverend Tim La Haye, one of the leading proponents of so-called Armageddon theology—someone, that is, who believes that the

Bible has revealed a precise scenario for the end of the world. It starts with the establishment of the state of Israel, includes the restoration of the Temple, a massive world war, the conversion of the Jews, and the transporting of true believers into heaven ('the rapture').

> 'The Bible says "No man knows the day or the hour",' said La Haye. 'But we can know the season. . . . One of the most important signs is that Israel and Russia are both dominant players on the world scene, just as the prophets said they would be 2,500 years ago. Russia was just a nothing power till our generation, and Israel was not even in the land'. He went on to quote a passage from Ezekiel about the invasion of Israel from the north. God, he believed, would supernaturally intervene to destroy Russia in the midst of its attack on Israel.

One could go on. It is perhaps appropriate to end with someone like La Haye, lest this more or less random and personal list of Bible readers should seem too apologetic or optimistic. It is not any part of my purpose to present a bland or anodyne view of the Bible. I am fully aware that the Bible has been used for purposes which for many are profoundly abhorrent, as well as in the cause of justice and liberation. It is true, for instance, that many members of the Dutch Reformed Churches, which supported apartheid, firmly believed that such policies were biblical and therefore theologically justified. At the same time, I am also aware of those engaged in the struggle against apartheid for whom the Bible was a source of moral and religious guidance and enlightenment. The fact that we have to contend with is that both sides could appeal to the Bible for enlightenment and guidance. The sheer diversity of the ways in which the Bible has been embodied in Jewish and Christian communities is both fascinating and disturbing.

The first part of this book will look at the long and complex process by which the Bible took a variety of forms and found its way to virtually every corner of the globe. Chapter 2 looks at some of the processes of tradition and composition that led to the final form of the biblical books as we know them today. Chapter 3 looks at the process whereby different books came to be included in the various Bibles which are now accepted as authoritative (canonical) by various religious communities, Jewish and Christian. Chapter 4 will look at the way that these Bibles were given physical form in particular formats and languages and how they were distributed around the world.

The rest of the book will focus on the different kinds of readings which the Bible has received in its long history. We shall look, in Chapter 5, at some of the readings of the Bible by believers, both Jews and Christians. Chapter 6 will look in more detail at the rich reception history of one particular book, Galatians. Chapter 7 concentrates on critical readings, mainly from the Reformation and the Enlightenment, which had radical effects on how the Bible was perceived. Chapter 8 discusses the role of the Bible in colonial history. Chapter 9 discusses its place in the world of politics. Chapter 10 looks at the part that the Bible has played in high and popular culture, and a summary concludes the book in Chapter 11.

The relationship between readers and text is, of course, a very complex one. Is it the diversity of the Bible which creates such a wide array of communities of readers? Or do different readers shape the Bible to their own ends and purposes, either literally, by deciding which books should or should not be included, or figuratively, by the different reading strategies which they adopt? How is one to respond to the variety of readings which the Bible is capable of bearing? These questions will accompany us through the book, as we investigate the various ways in which the Bible has been read and lived out.

At this point I should enter a strong disclaimer. I cannot possibly speak for all readers of the Bible, or even give a fair selection of different points of view about the Bible. For a start, as Chapter 3 illustrates, there is no such thing as 'the Bible': there are a significant number of Bibles, which differ both in the books included and in the order in which those books occur. In the second place, the Bible belongs to a wide range of religious (and not so religious) communities the world over. I am a white, male, European, English-born, Anglican Christian who taught New Testament in a Scottish university. Universities are, generally, open-minded places, where a certain internationalism is fostered. We were fortunate in the stream of overseas students and visitors who enriched our collegiate life. But while all of this helps to enlarge one's sense of who one is, I cannot pretend that it enables me wholly to transcend the social and cultural mix that, in part at least, makes me who I am. I belong to a particular community of readers, albeit one which has links with other such communities. But we can only do our reading and thinking within our own particular context, facing the questions which are of particular urgency for us, reflecting the kinds of deep-seated beliefs and assumptions which are ours. Some of the questions which concern me from my perspective will indeed be global questions, of concern to many communities around the world. Even so, I will inevitably reflect on such questions from my perspective. I will try to be as open as I can about such slants, but readers should beware!

Chapter 2
How the biblical books were written

This is an impossibly optimistic title for a short chapter in a very short introduction. Nevertheless, we need to say something about the processes by which the books we have in our Bibles reached their present form. This chapter will take just a few examples, to stand for the very rich material that the Bible contains.

First, a word about the time span during which the texts were written. The earliest portions of the Old Testament probably date from the 10th or 11th century BCE (the poem in Judges 5), while the latest (the book of Daniel) comes from the Maccabean period of the 2nd century BCE. The time span for the New Testament is much shorter. The earliest of Paul's letters stems from *c.*50 CE; the majority of the rest of the texts fall within the 1st century. The latest date seriously put forward for any of the NT books is around the mid-2nd century for 2 Peter. This means that the biblical texts were produced over a period in which the living conditions of the writers—political, cultural, economic, and ecological—varied enormously. There are texts which reflect a nomadic existence, texts from people with an established monarchy and Temple cult, texts from exile, texts born out of fierce oppression by foreign rulers, courtly texts, texts from wandering charismatic preachers, texts from those who give themselves the airs of sophisticated Hellenistic writers. It is a time span which encompasses the compositions of Homer, Plato, Aristotle, Thucydides, Sophocles,

Caesar, Cicero, and Catullus. It is a period which sees the rise and fall of the Assyrian empire (12th to 7th century) and of the Persian empire (6th to 4th century), Alexander's campaigns (336–326 BCE), the rise of Rome and its achieving domination of the Mediterranean (4th century to the founding of the Principate, 27 BCE), the destruction of the Jerusalem Temple (70 CE), and the extension of Roman rule to parts of Scotland (84 CE).

Orality and literacy

One thing that these texts, so widely separated in time, have in common is their location in a culture in which writing was highly valued, even if its practice was still largely in the hands of specialists. The period of the composition of the earliest biblical texts broadly corresponds with the advance from cuneiform writing and hieroglyphs to the use of an alphabet. In cuneiform writing, whole words are represented by signs incised into clay tablets by a wedge-shaped instrument. Hieroglyphs, which represented sounds or ideas associated with words, were used for monumental inscriptions or written by pen on papyrus. In the earliest alphabets, which originate with the Phoenicians, consonants are inscribed in ink on papyrus or some such suitable material. This was more flexible and portable and made it possible to produce much longer texts. Texts in the new alphabet could be written on scrolls, usually made of leather, and could encompass all the sixty-six chapters of Isaiah. The later development of the codex (roughly corresponding to our present book format) made for greater ease of reference and portability. A codex would permit the inclusion of all four Gospels within the same covers, producing a volume about two and a half times the length of this book. Its use as a medium for literary texts, pioneered by the early Christians, dates from the 1st century CE. It became standard from about the 4th century.

The development of new techniques of recording language was one of the most remarkable technological features of this time, comparable in importance to the development of the printing press in the 15th century. However, for the most part, culture during the biblical period remained oral. Written texts were mostly communicated by being read aloud: the majority of those who received the texts would have heard rather than read them. Most of the material we now have in written form, whether legal, prophetic, proverbial, poetic, or narrative, will have started out in oral form and only subsequently been committed to writing. So, for example, prophetic oracles were delivered orally by the prophet, committed to memory by the prophet's disciples, and then later written down. Between the initial oracles, their subsequent writing down, their collection together with other similar material, and their taking form as a prophetic book, a period of several centuries may have elapsed, as with the book of Isaiah. Even where texts were produced by one person, as were the Pauline epistles, they were mostly dictated to a scribe, though Paul on occasion added his own greetings: 'See what large letters I make when I am writing to you in my own hand!' (Galatians 6:11).

Throughout the period of the composition of the Bible, orality and literacy are closely interrelated. This is reflected in the fact that there are different degrees of literateness among the texts: some come from literary, often courtly, circles; others are much closer to the oral recitation of narratives and discourses. The earliest narratives in the Hebrew Bible, as John Barton has suggested, are written in a style which is similar to that of Icelandic sagas and are closer to the style of oral narrative. In the Gospels, Mark's Gospel, generally agreed to be the earliest of the four, is also the least literate, both in the roughness of its Greek style and in the closeness of its contents to the oral tradition of stories and sayings about Jesus. Luke, by contrast, tells us quite clearly that he is writing as a Greek historian who has sifted his sources carefully (Luke 1:1–4). His style is noticeably literary, echoing the Greek translation of the Hebrew scriptures.

The Bible's literary world

Within this overall context of literacy and orality, how did the biblical texts acquire written form? The biblical writers would certainly have approached their task very differently from a modern novelist. The novelist is in large measure in control of her material, creating a literary whole from her imagination and experience, drawing on literary forms, allusions, and traditions as she will. By contrast, the ancient writers of religious texts are much more constrained by the deposits of the past, whether oral or literary. They are as much compilers as they are composers of texts.

One only has to read the opening chapters of Genesis to sense what a different literary world one has entered. In chapter 1 we learn how God created the world over six days and rested on the seventh. The narrative starts with a description of chaos and darkness and builds up, through the creation of the heavenly bodies, land and seas, plants and animals, to its climax in the creation of man and woman. 'God created man in his own image, in the image of God he created him; male and female he created them' (Genesis 1:27). The story stresses the goodness of creation, its worth in and of itself, before man and woman even come on the scene. This is not to deny the strong sense of human domination over the created world which is expressed in verse 28. Even so, there is a limit to human domination. Both human beings and animals are strictly vegetarian. Only after the flood (Genesis 9:3–4) are human beings permitted to eat meat. The chapter finishes with God resting from his labours, contemplating everything that he has made, 'and behold, it was very good'.

So far there is nothing very remarkable to alert us to the different literary world which we have entered. But in 2:4 the story starts again, and in a rather different form. The story is differently structured: the device of days which was used in chapter 1 is absent. The order of events is very different: after a brief account of the creation of the heavens and the earth, God causes a mist to come up and water the earth and, before any other creatures, creates man/Adam (the Hebrew 'Adam' is both the word for 'human being' and a name). But, while the term is generic, Adam is a male and very much on his own. The rest of the story is then structured around God's provision of succour and support for him. First, God creates a garden, with plants and trees for food, with the exception of the tree of knowledge of good and evil. Then he creates the animals to be Adam's companions. Not even these are enough. Finally God puts Adam to sleep and creates from his rib a woman, and Adam is content, for the time being at least. The story finishes with the man and woman together, blissfully unaware of their nakedness.

The differences in these two accounts are striking. Their style is different: chapter 2 is written in the saga style; chapter 1 is written in a priestly style 'rehearsing set pieces of ritualized events' (Barton, *A History of the Bible*). The second account represents God in frankly human terms, places human beings at the centre of creation, and, in its story of woman's creation out of Adam's rib, vividly symbolizes women's subordination to men. Like a sculptor, God models man out of dust; like some kind of Frankenstein, he puts man to sleep and takes out a rib and turns it into a woman. How different from the loftier account of God's agency in chapter 1: 'And God said, "Let there be light"; and there was light' (1:3), a motif which is repeated throughout the chapter. Again, chapter 2 makes the whole purpose of creation rotate around man's (*sic*!) needs. Everything is put there for man's purpose and without man nothing will be brought into existence. In chapter 1, human beings are indeed the crowning glory of creation, but are still very much a part of the whole process. Finally, chapter 2's account of human creation is unashamedly male oriented: man's creation is put first and everything subsequent depends on him. Woman's creation comes right at the end, a last resort, which rapidly goes badly wrong.

One final difference, not apparent from the English translation. In Genesis 1 God is referred to by the Hebrew *'elohim,* which is actually a plural form. In Genesis 2, he is additionally referred to as YHWH (probably to be read as Yahweh, but in the first scrolls only consonants were written down).

That is to say, we have here two versions of the same story, using different terminology for no less important a character than God, and containing a considerable measure of inconsistency over the order of creation, over men and women's relation to it, and indeed over the question of man and woman's relation to each other.

Such phenomena are found throughout the Bible. In the first five books, there are different, and somewhat contradictory, accounts of the flood (cf. Genesis 7:2, 3 with 6:19; 7:8, 9, 15), Abraham's migration (Genesis 12:1–4a; 12:4b–5), God's covenant with Abraham (Genesis 15 and 17), the manna and quail in the wilderness (Exodus 16:2–3, 6–35a; Numbers 11:4–34), the Ten Commandments (Exodus 20:1–17; 34:10–28; Deuteronomy 5:6–21), and the dietary rules prohibiting the eating of certain animals (Leviticus 11 and Deuteronomy 14). There are frequent differences in terminology. In some accounts, Sinai is the mountain of the covenant (e.g. Exodus 19:1; 24:16); in others it is Horeb (Deuteronomy 4:10; 5:2). Some stories favour certain Hebrew words, for example relating to dying, the plague, the congregation, which occur rarely, if at all, in the parallel stories. Not only do parallel versions of stories exist but the fact that they can be sorted into groups with a largely consistent use of certain terms suggests that the different groups have different origins and history.

What are we to make of all this? The classic scholarly view was that the biblical stories are taken from four different written sources and that these were brought together over the course of time to form the first five books of the Bible as a composite work. Based on the specific linguistic usage in the suggested sources,

Box 1 Classic view of the sources for the five books of the Pentateuch: Genesis, Exodus, Leviticus, Numbers, Deuteronomy

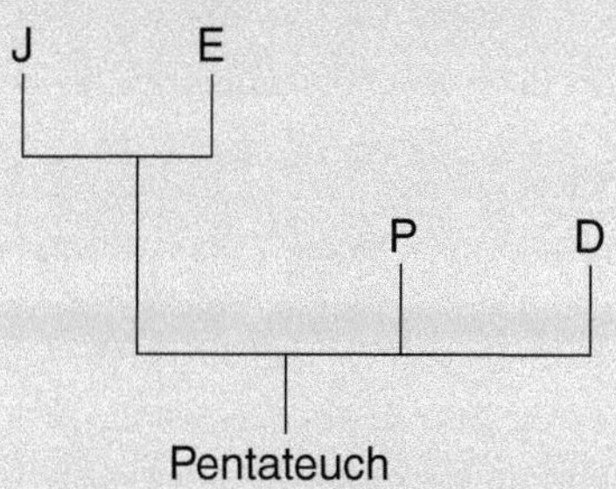

they are known as J, the Jahwist source (from the German transliteration of the Hebrew YHWH), E, the Elohist source, P, the priestly source, and D, the Deuteronomistic source. More recently, scholars have questioned whether a clear division can be drawn between J and E. The earliest material goes back to the 11th century. The final compilation dates from the 5th century, and may include revisions reflecting overall the views of P. Thus the Pentateuch (or Torah, as it is known by Jews) comprises material composed over six centuries, put together to give a comprehensive picture of the creation of the world and of God's dealings with his peoples, specifically with the people of Israel (Box 1).

It is not only the books of the Old Testament which have their origins in a variety of oral and literary traditions. The same is true of the Gospels. The Gospels offer four accounts of Jesus's life, death, and resurrection, with interesting differences of perspective and detail, though also with considerable agreement. In the case of the first three, Matthew, Mark, and Luke, the agreements are remarkable. They not only agree about the order of many events and in much of the detail of what occurred, they also agree in the overall literary structure of the narrative, even in sentence structure, choice of words, and grammatical forms. These linguistic agreements are so striking that one has to conclude that there is literary dependence of one kind or another: someone has been copying someone else.

Take, for example, the story of the calling of a tax-collector.

Matthew 9:9–13

As Jesus was walking along, he saw a man called Matthew sitting at the tax booth; and he said to him, 'Follow me.' And he got up and followed him. And as he sat at dinner in the house, many tax-collectors and sinners came and were sitting with him and his disciples. When the Pharisees saw this, they said to his disciples, 'Why does your teacher eat with tax-collectors and sinners?' But when he heard this, he said, 'Those who are well have no need of a physician, but those who are sick. Go and learn what this means, "I desire mercy, not sacrifice." For I have come to call not the righteous but sinners.'

Mark 2:13–17

And as he was walking along, he saw Levi son of Alphaeus sitting at the tax booth, and he said to him, 'Follow me.' And he got up and followed him. And as he sat at dinner in his house, many tax-collectors and sinners were also sitting with Jesus and his disciples—for there were many who followed him. When the scribes of the Pharisees saw that he was eating with sinners and tax-collectors, they said to his disciples, 'Why does he eat with tax-collectors and sinners?' When Jesus heard this, he said to them, 'Those who are well have no need of a physician, but those who are sick; I have come to call not the righteous, but sinners.'

Luke 5:27–32

After this he went out and saw a tax-collector named Levi, sitting at the tax booth; and he said to him, 'Follow me.' And he got up, left everything, and followed him. Then Levi gave a great banquet for him in his house; and there was a large crowd of tax collectors and others sitting at the table with them. The Pharisees and their scribes were complaining to his disciples, saying, 'Why do you eat and drink with tax-collectors and sinners?' Jesus answered, 'Those who are well have no need of a physician, but those who are sick; I have come to call not the righteous but sinners to repentance.'

It's an instructive exercise to compare these three versions, underlining the words that they share in common and noting the sometimes minor, but significant, differences which there are. The difference between Mark and Matthew's version: 'I have come to call not the righteous but sinners' (in the context of a story about Jesus calling people to follow him), and Luke's 'I have come to call not the righteous but sinners *to repentance*' is quite significant.

Scholars have expended much energy and wit in trying to work out who was copying from whom. The usual, though by no means undisputed, view is that Mark wrote first, and that Matthew and Luke both used Mark and another source consisting mainly of sayings attributed to Jesus and referred to as Q. This then allows the historian of early Christianity to reconstruct different theological perspectives associated with the different Gospels and also with Q. But that is not quite the end of the story. What about the earliest Gospel, Mark? Where did he get his material from? Behind Mark must lie oral traditions which he collected and put into some kind of order. Similarly, the material ascribed to Q (broadly the sayings which Matthew and Luke have in common) may also have been in oral, not written, form.

Scholars have attempted to reconstruct something of the history of the oral traditions behind the Gospels, but the results have not been too encouraging. The period of transmission is short: less than forty years passed between the death of Jesus and the writing of Mark's Gospel. This means that there was little time for oral traditions to assume fixed form, though it is likely that there was an extended oral narrative of the last days of Jesus, which was probably used in Christian worship and formed the basis of the various accounts of Jesus's death (the Passion narratives) in the Gospels. Even so, it is difficult to know which elements of Mark's Gospel (or indeed of the hypothetical Q) come from the tradition and which from Mark himself.

Nevertheless, it is likely that stories and sayings about Jesus circulated in varying oral forms before they were written down. The Gospels, like the Hebrew Bible, have their roots in an oral culture. Yet while they resemble the Hebrew Bible in that respect, there is also an impressive rush to literacy in the Gospels. Four major literary accounts of the life, death, and resurrection of Jesus within a period of around forty years is a clear indication of the growing importance of literary production in all levels of society in the 1st-century Mediterranean world. It is also indicative of the early Christians' desire to be part of that society, despite their beliefs in an imminent and dramatic end to the world as they knew it.

To sum up: many of the books of the Bible are not the work of one author, written over a period of a few years; rather they are compilations which reflect communal traditions which may go back many centuries. Even in the case of the New Testament, where the individual books each have their own author, the Gospels are still in an important sense communal productions, which preserve the traditions of the earliest Christians.

Yet, even though the writings of the Bible have deep roots in an oral culture and tradition, they are also clearly literary works. In the first place, they use literary forms and conventions. The Bible contains a great variety of such forms. The Hebrew Bible is traditionally divided into three parts: the Torah, the Prophets, and the Writings. The Torah (or Pentateuch) comprises the first five books and contains a mixture of narratives and legal texts. In some sections narrative predominates (Genesis, Exodus, and Numbers), in others legal material (Leviticus and Deuteronomy). Deuteronomy is cast as the last testament of Moses to the people, prior to his death and the entry of the people into the Land under Joshua. The Prophets contains prophetic books with both narrative and prophetic oracles, preceded by the histories of Joshua, Judges, Samuel, and Kings and Chronicles. These latter books contain masterpieces of story-telling, but also construct a history of the people with, again, distinctive theological perspectives. The Writings contains a mixture of psalms, proverbial material, and more historical books.

The New Testament books, composed in less than 200 years, (Box 2), add a number of forms to this: gospels, resembling contemporary biographies or 'Lives'; letters, which vary from the fairly short personal communication (Philemon) to Paul's elaborate treatise of sixteen chapters in Romans; acts, a form recording the deeds of famous figures; and an apocalypse, Revelation, a contemporary form which enjoyed considerable popularity in 1st-century Judaism.

The writers and compilers of the Bible, that is to say, used a variety of literary forms in which to cast their works. Within the tradition of biblical writing and compilation such literary forms became influential and constrained the way in which the books were written. Even the gospel form, which may, as a particular variation of the contemporary Life, be ascribed to Mark, was immediately emulated by the other canonical evangelists and by many others whose works were never included in the canon. The Bible both drew on and created literary traditions and forms.

Literary allusions within the Bible

This consciousness of working within a literary tradition is reflected in the way the writers refer back to earlier books in the Bible. It is natural that, in recording the lives and deeds of the great figures of their people's history, writers should make comparisons. Even though, as Deuteronomy says, 'Never since has there arisen a prophet in Israel like Moses' (Deuteronomy 34:10),

Box 2 Approximate dates of New Testament books and contemporary writers

	New Testament books	*Contemporary Greek and Latin writers*
49	1 Thessalonians	Philo of Alexandria, Jewish Hellenistic philosopher (15 BCE–50 CE)
52–4	Galatians	
	1 Corinthians	Plutarch, Greek historian, philosopher, and writer (46–120)
55–6	2 Corinthians	Epictetus, Greek Stoic philosopher
	Romans	(50–138)
60–2	Philemon	Juvenal, Roman satirical writer (58–138)
	Philippians	Seneca, Roman Stoic philosopher, commits suicide on Nero's order (65)
68–70	Mark	Petronius, Roman satirical novelist, commits suicide (66)
75–90	Matthew, Luke, Acts	Martial, Roman epigrammatic poet (40–104)
90s	John, 1, 2, 3 John, Jude	
95–6	Revelation (41–100)	
100–130	2 Peter	

Other books (Colossians, Ephesians, Hebrews, 1 and 2 Timothy, Titus, James) can be dated broadly in the last three decades of the 1st century CE.

that does not deter later writers from underscoring the point. When Joshua, commissioned by Moses to lead the people into the Promised Land, comes with the Ark of the Covenant to the Jordan, the allusions to the Crossing of the Red Sea are clear. In both cases the people camp before the waters and then move out in the morning. There is a miraculous parting of the waters, so that the waters form a wall (Exodus 14:21–2), 'stand in a single heap' (Joshua 3:13, 16). In all this Joshua does as Moses has told him, and the people stand in awe of him, 'as they had stood in awe of Moses' (4:14). Similar points of comparison can be made between the story of Gideon's call in Judges 6 and Moses' call in Exodus 3. Such comparisons are developed further in later retellings.

The process is continued in the retelling of these stories in extra-biblical Hebrew and Greek literature and in the New Testament. The infancy stories in Matthew contain quotations and more indirect allusions to the Moses birth story. When in Matthew 2:19–20 the angel of the Lord appears to Joseph in Egypt to tell him it is safe to return home after fleeing from Herod, his words closely echo God's words to Moses in Midian, Exodus 4:19–21.

What these brief examples show is a living religious tradition where the textual tradition is in dialogue with itself. What is accepted as sacred truth in one book is taken up and interpreted in later writings. The range of this kind of literary interplay is much wider than can be illustrated here. The figure of Moses runs through the narratives of the Bible, shaping the way the stories are told, used as a standard by which to judge subsequent characters in the narrative. Similarly the story of the Exodus, the desert wanderings, and the capture of the Land will return again to shape legal, prophetic, and liturgical material. The great events of the past as told in sacred scripture inevitably affect the way the present is experienced and the future dreamt of. The prophecies of Isaiah draw on the theme of the entry into the Land after the desert wanderings to encourage those in exile to hope for return, to look for the glorious restoration of Israel, when all nations will flock to pay homage to Zion, to the restored glory of Temple and nation (see Isaiah 40:1–11, 60:1–14).

The same visions shaped the beliefs of Jews at the time of Christ's birth. The Qumran sectarians, the authors of the Dead Sea Scrolls, had established a tightly regulated community in the Judaean desert in the 1st century CE; following Isaiah 40:3, 'In the wilderness prepare the way of the Lord', they saw their going out into the desert as a preparation for the final restoration of Israel and the renewal of the Temple. Similarly, in Mark's Gospel, John the Baptist opens the Gospel by proclaiming 'the way of the Lord'. He is in turn pointing to his own baptizing in the desert, which is to prepare the way for Jesus, the stronger one who will come after him to baptize with the holy Spirit and with fire.

It is interesting to reflect on the very different contexts in which these texts were shaped. The text from Isaiah comes from the period of Israel's exile in Babylon. It promises to those whose lives have been uprooted a return to the Land and to their former glories. Indeed their glory will be greater: all nations will come to acknowledge the glory of the Lord. By contrast, the Qumran sectarians lived in inner exile in the Land, seeing both the Roman occupying forces and the Temple priests as being ruled over by the spirit of darkness. Their world has again been overturned by foreign forces who have robbed them of their independence and undermined their religious traditions and the religious leaders of the nation. They too embrace the prophetic hope for a return to the founding moments of Jewish history; however, they look not for a physical return from exile, but for the overthrow of the occupying forces and a restoration and renewal of the Temple and its priesthood.

In the Gospel of Mark, the sense of these ancient prophecies is extended still further. Mark, writing for a persecuted community of Gentile Christians in Rome, is in no way concerned with the renewal or restoration of Israel and the Jerusalem Temple. For him the 'way of the Lord' leads from John's baptizing in the desert via Jesus's ministry of preaching, healing, and exorcizing to Jerusalem, where Jesus is crucified and the veil of the Temple is torn. The disciples are then told to return to Galilee, from where they will go out to preach the gospel to all nations. The problems faced by Mark's Gentile community, barbaric public torture and execution, are no longer peculiar to a particular nation. As such their resolution can no longer be conceived in terms of national restoration. For Mark, the resolution of these problems lies in Jesus's binding of Satan and his calling people to be with him (3:14) and to preach this good news to all nations (13:10).

A living oral and literary tradition

I have tried in this chapter to give some impression of the way in which the biblical books were composed. In particular I have been keen to stress their genesis in a period which saw the rise of literature but which was nevertheless still in many ways an oral culture. This marks the Bible as a collection of texts which has deep roots in the oral traditions of Jews and Christians. These texts were only gradually written down and this process itself would have gone through several stages. The books we now have may have been based on or incorporate other literary collections and documents.

Oral traditions, once written down, can influence the creation of further literary works, or the editing of new oral material. The earlier works of the Bible exert their influence on later writing and at the same time are reworked and even subverted by later writing. The tradition, oral or literary, is a dynamic and sometimes contentious one. It certainly does not speak with one voice, but the different voices speak the same language. They pick up phrases and motifs, they share a common stock of images and ideas which they republish in sometimes strikingly different ways.

It is a lively and wide-ranging exchange, with stories and histories, debates about laws and regulations, proverbs and sayings, letters and visions. Such texts contain a rich vocabulary through which people in different situations and at different times may attempt to come to terms with their experiences of well-being or of suffering and oppression. These texts provide a rich source of legal, social, and political wisdom by which people may seek to order their affairs, to strengthen the nation, and to live with their neighbours. They are also the stuff of dreams. The great events of the past, of deliverance from bondage and of heroic perseverance in the desert, may be recreated in the future. New worlds may emerge which mirror the past and its glories in wholly surprising ways. The process of reappropriation and reworking of texts which occurs within the biblical writings continues, as we shall see, in the subsequent history of their reception within Jewish and Christian communities.

Chapter 3
The making of the Bible

The many names of the Bible

So far I have been speaking fairly freely about 'the Bible', without asking what might be meant by that expression. The word itself is derived from the Greek *biblia*, which is simply the plural form of *biblion*, book. The singularity of the expression 'the Bible' conceals a sense of plurality in its etymological roots. The Bible is a collection of books. Which books and why?

The *Oxford English Dictionary* defines the Bible as follows: 'the Christian scriptures, consisting of the Old and New Testaments; the Jewish scriptures, consisting of the Torah or Law, the Prophets, and the Hagiographa or Writings'. This reflects the history of the term, which starts out life as a specifically Christian term and then passes into wider usage; and it indicates the striking difference in content which different books known as the Bible may hold.

First, a word about nomenclature. These collections of books have not always been known as the Bible. Jewish sacred writings have had many names. The most common are 'scripture', 'the scriptures', 'the sacred scriptures', 'the books', 'the 24 books', 'the Law, the Prophets and the Writings', 'Tanak' (an acronym based on the initial Hebrew letters of the words for the different sections of scripture—Torah, Nebi'im, Ketubim), and 'mikra' (literally, 'what is read [aloud]'). The last two were established by the Middle Ages. Names such as 'the Jewish Bible' and 'the Hebrew Bible' are much more recent, though their precise origin is difficult to pin down. They have quite recently become the subject of considerable attention in departments of religious studies, where titles like 'the chair of Old Testament' seem inappropriate in a multicultural or multifaith context.

Christian usage has its roots in these Jewish names. In the New Testament writings we find references to 'scripture' and 'the scriptures', where the singular refers either to particular passages (sometimes 'this scripture', e.g. Mark 12:10) or to scripture as a whole (e.g. Romans 4:3). This latter use is probably derived from the Greek translation of the Hebrew scriptures, known as the Septuagint. Here Hebrew expressions like 'by the word of YHWH' are translated 'by the word of God in scripture' (e.g. 1 Chronicles 15:15). This usage is sustained in the subsequent tradition, and in Latin, as *sacra scriptura,* is standard in the works of Thomas Aquinas in the Middle Ages. It remains a favoured way of referring to the Bible within Roman Catholic theological circles.

Sometimes in the New Testament, the Greek *biblion* (book) is used for the book of the Law (Galatians 3:10; Hebrews 9:19): here the writers again follow the usage of the Septuagint. However, other 1st-century Jewish writers in Greek, notably Josephus and Philo, predominantly use the plural *biblia.* This usage becomes standard in church circles from the later 4th century. Then in the Middle Ages the Latin borrowed word *biblia* comes to be treated as a singular expression which is reflected in other European languages: *the bible, la bible, la biblia, die Bibel,* etc.

To summarize: the term Bible, referring to a collection of sacred texts, is first used for the Christian scriptures, in their different versions. Only later is it used of Jewish scriptures to distinguish the Hebrew from the Christian scriptures. Thus 'the Bible', in most recent usage, is ambiguous: it may refer either to the Jewish or the Christian Bibles, in their various forms.

Now we need to consider how these collections were made and how such collections varied. What kind of diversity has the process of collecting and fixing the scriptures of the different Jewish and Christian communities produced?

The making of the Jewish canon: the Hebrew Bible and its Greek version

The process of collecting and fixing the scriptures of a particular community is often referred to as the canonization of scripture. The Greek word *kanon* means rod or reed, and, by extension, rule or measure. To create a canon of sacred writings is to create a collection which will be binding for the community for which it is intended. The process is complex and for both Jewish and Christian scriptures complicated by the fact that they were soon being produced in different languages. Collection and translation were closely connected. We will look first at the formation of the Hebrew Bible and then at its Greek version, the Septuagint.

The formation of the Hebrew Bible

As we have already seen, the writings which together form the Hebrew Bible were composed over a long period, some 900 years. Their collection together as authoritative books for their communities was also a lengthy process. Simplifying, we may say that the earlier books of the Bible were fixed first: the books of the Law and the books which record the story of Israel's entry into the Land and its subsequent history. Next came the prophetic books; and finally what were known as the 'writings': psalms, songs, proverbs, and more meditative (and sometimes apparently sceptical) writings. The Law was probably canonized around 400

BCE and the Prophets around 200 BCE. It is much less clear when the final section, the Writings, was fixed.

This impression of the relative fixity of the first two sections, the Law and the Prophets, and the considerable fluidity of the third is confirmed by the biblical manuscripts found among the Dead Sea Scrolls. Here we have the contents (often in a very fragmentary state) of the library of a 1st-century Jewish sect. It contains at least parts of all the books currently contained in the Hebrew Bible, except the book of Esther. There was therefore already a considerable consensus about which books should be included in the Jewish sacred scriptures. Other features however suggest a significant measure of fluidity at this period. The copies of the Psalms found at Qumran contain significant variations from the later canonical versions: thirty-five we might expect are missing, including Psalm 110, and there are a considerable number of 'additions'. The library, alongside writings specific to the community itself, also contained a number of writings not in the present Hebrew Bible but which are in the Septuagint. Some (e.g. the book of Jubilees, a retelling of the Genesis narrative, with theological ideas close to some of those found in the sect's own writings) remain outside the canons of either the Jewish or the Christian communities. Jubilees is however found in the Ethiopian canon.

It looks, then, as if the final shape of the Hebrew Bible emerged some time after the destruction of the Temple in Jerusalem in 70 CE. How then did the process of canonization work? Who, in the absence of the Temple priesthood, had authority to proclaim works canonical? Was it the group of Pharisees who, according to tradition, gathered around Johanan ben Zakkai at Jamnia (Yavneh)? Many now doubt that this grouping would have had the kind of authority required to command recognition throughout Jewish communities in the Mediterranean and the Middle East. More likely, the process was gradual. Communities came to recognize the value of some writings and the dangers of others.

Those containing fierier visions of cosmic battles and the overthrow of Jewish enemies would have been regarded with caution in the light of the painful experiences of defeat at the hands of the Romans, both in the Jewish War (66–73), and in the Bar Kochba revolt (132–5). The book of Enoch, found in the Qumran library, was excluded, while others, like the book of Daniel, were retained, possibly because they had gained wider currency before the wars. Probably there was no firmly agreed canon until well into the 2nd century CE.

Nor is this the end of the story. The text of the canonical writings at this point was written in unpointed Hebrew (and, in a few parts, Aramaic). Let me explain. The Hebrew alphabet is made up of twenty-four consonants (though some of them can be pressed into service as vowels). Words are thus represented by clusters of consonants. It was not until the development of Greek that an alphabet was devised which contained vowels pure and simple. This clearly meant that it was possible to disagree about the way in which a cluster of consonants should be read. Not only might there be different ways of supplying the 'missing' vowels, it would also be possible when copying manuscripts to regroup the consonants to form different clusters and therefore quite different words. This leaves a good deal of room for scribal error. From the 6th century CE, these ambiguities were addressed by the Masoretes, scholars who created a system of adding points to the consonantal text to represent the vowels which should be supplied.

The Greek translation: the Septuagint

From the late 4th century BCE, after Alexander's successful campaigns, Greek became the principal means of communication for much of the world inhabited by Jews. Jewish communities lived all across the Mediterranean and the Middle East. Many Jews grew up in Greek-speaking cities like Alexandria and went to Greek schools. Many no longer spoke Hebrew. From the middle of the 3rd century BCE translations into Greek began to be made of the Pentateuch, with the other books following over a period of centuries. That is to say, the process of translation into Greek occurred at the same time as the canon of the Hebrew Bible was being fixed.

The Greek translation is generally referred to as the Septuagint. This derives from the Latin *septuaginta*, meaning seventy. The Epistle of Aristeas (mid-2nd century BCE) relates that seventy-two elders translated the Pentateuch into Greek at the request of a King Ptolemy of Egypt. They were so well looked after and so industrious that they completed the task in seventy-two days. Although this story is generally regarded as legendary, the term has stuck, even in scholarly circles. The work is often referred to by the Roman numerals LXX.

There are a number of intriguing features about this parallel process of translation and canonization. In the first place, there are substantial differences between the Hebrew and Greek versions of particular books, notably of Jeremiah, which is an eighth shorter in the Greek. (Hebrew texts of Jeremiah found at Qumran are closer to the Greek than to the canonical Hebrew text.) Secondly, there are substantial differences in the number of books included, both between different versions of the Septuagint and between the Septuagint and the Hebrew Bible. Generally speaking, 1 Esdras, Wisdom of Solomon, Sirach, Judith, Tobit, Baruch, the Letter of Jeremiah, 1–4 Maccabees, and the Psalms of Solomon are not found in the Hebrew Bible but are included in the Septuagint. Thirdly, there are variations in order. The threefold division of the Hebrew Bible is abandoned in the Septuagint. It appears that there was no clear division made between the Pentateuch and the rest of the historical books. Thereafter there is little agreement in the order of the books: some manuscripts place the psalms and wisdom literature before the prophets (as in Protestant Bibles); others reverse this order. In some versions, the book of Daniel is included among the major prophets; in others it is among the minor ones.

The Christian Old Testament

While the Septuagint started life as a translation for Jews living in the Diaspora, it was subsequently taken up by the Christian community as the medium through which the Old Testament (as it came to be called) was known in the Church. Thus from the start the Christian Bible included more books than the equivalent Hebrew collections. The language of the Septuagint influenced many of the writers of the New Testament. Not until St Jerome translated the Christian Bible into Latin in the late 4th/early 5th century was the standing of the Septuagint questioned. Jerome used an early form of the text of our present Hebrew Bible and went to considerable lengths to learn Hebrew. His translation introduced a strong element of stability into the text of the Christian Old Testament in its official Latin form, known as the Vulgate.

However, the history of the Christian Old Testament does not stop here. The translation of the Bible into Latin marks the beginning of a parting of the ways between Western Latin-speaking Christianity and Eastern Christianity, which spoke Greek, Syriac, Coptic, Ethiopic, and other languages. The Bibles of the Eastern Churches vary considerably: the Ethiopic Orthodox canon includes eighty-one books and contains many apocalyptic texts, such as were found at Qumran and subsequently excluded from the Jewish canon. As a general rule, one can say that the Orthodox Churches follow the Septuagint in including more books in their Old Testaments than are in the Jewish canon.

The same was true of the West until the time of the Reformation, when there was a renewal of interest in the Hebrew text of the Old Testament. In this they followed Jerome who, as the translators of the Authorized or King James Version put it, translated 'out of the very fountains themselves', that is to say, the Hebrew text. Allied with this goes a much greater respect for the books of the Hebrew

Bible than for those found only in the Septuagint. These books are clearly separated from the books of the Old and New Testaments and referred to as 'The books called Apocrypha'. The expression 'apocrypha', a plural noun from the Greek adjective meaning 'hidden' or 'obscure', was introduced by the German Reformer Carlstadt in 1520, with the implication that these books were reserved for the discerning. The Reformers regarded them with suspicion because the Second Book of Maccabees included prayers for the dead (2 Maccabees 12:43–4), a Catholic practice they rejected. This mistrust is reflected in the lectionaries in the Anglican Book of Common Prayer, where only rarely are passages to be publicly read from the Apocrypha, and then mostly from Ecclesiasticus (ben Sirach) or Baruch or the Wisdom of Solomon. The Roman Catholic Church, by contrast, reaffirmed the authority of these books, referring to them as 'deutero-canonical', that is, secondarily canonical. In a further twist to the story, from the 1820s onwards it became a widespread practice among (Protestant) Bible societies to print Bibles without the Apocrypha at all. More recent ecumenical editions of the Bible, like the Common Bible, have restored the deutero-canonical books.

The Christian New Testament

The process of the formation of the Christian canon of the New Testament (i.e. of writings which have a specifically Christian origin) is not all that dissimilar from that by which the Hebrew scriptures came to be canonized.

In the early days of Christianity, there were of course no scriptures written by Christians. 'Scripture' for the early Christians was what they would subsequently come to call the Old Testament. Nor is it likely that the first Christian writings were composed as scripture. Once, however, Christian writings began to be seen as scripture themselves, they needed to be distinguished from the older canonical writings. The terms Old Testament and New Testament were introduced during the 2nd century. Originally they referred respectively to the covenants which God had made with the people of Israel through Moses and with the Church through Jesus. As applied to Christian writings, the name indicated that these were books belonging to the old or new covenant, not that the books themselves were the covenants. Later of course the terms came to refer to the books themselves, as on the title page of the King James Bible: 'The Holy Bible conteyning the Old Testament, and the New' (see Figure 1).

How did a selection of early Christian writings come to be recognized as authoritative for the Church? The purposes of the books chosen are varied: Paul's letters were occasional communications to churches around the Mediterranean (or exceptionally to an individual, Philemon), addressing specific matters of belief and practice. They were in some ways a substitute for his own presence, offering advice, exhortation, argument, admonition, scolding. They were an exercise of authority on Paul's part and were probably intended to be read out at meetings of the congregation. From the start, they claimed apostolic authority and had a role in the worship of the communities to which they were addressed. Some of the other letters, notably the so-called Catholic epistles (James, 1 and 2 Peter, 1–3 John), may have been intended for wider circulation, as indeed was the book of Revelation, though this is strictly an apocalypse (an account of visions and revelations) rather than a letter.

It is rather more difficult to say what the purposes behind the writing of the Gospels were. Some have thought that they, like Paul's letters, were written to address particular issues within their own communities. Matthew's Gospel, it has been suggested, was written in the aftermath of the destruction of the Temple to legitimize the position of his Christian Jewish congregation in relation to the dominant Jewish group, the heirs to the Pharisaic tradition. Thus Jesus is presented as a teacher who fulfils the Law and the prophets (5:17) and the Pharisees are attacked as blind

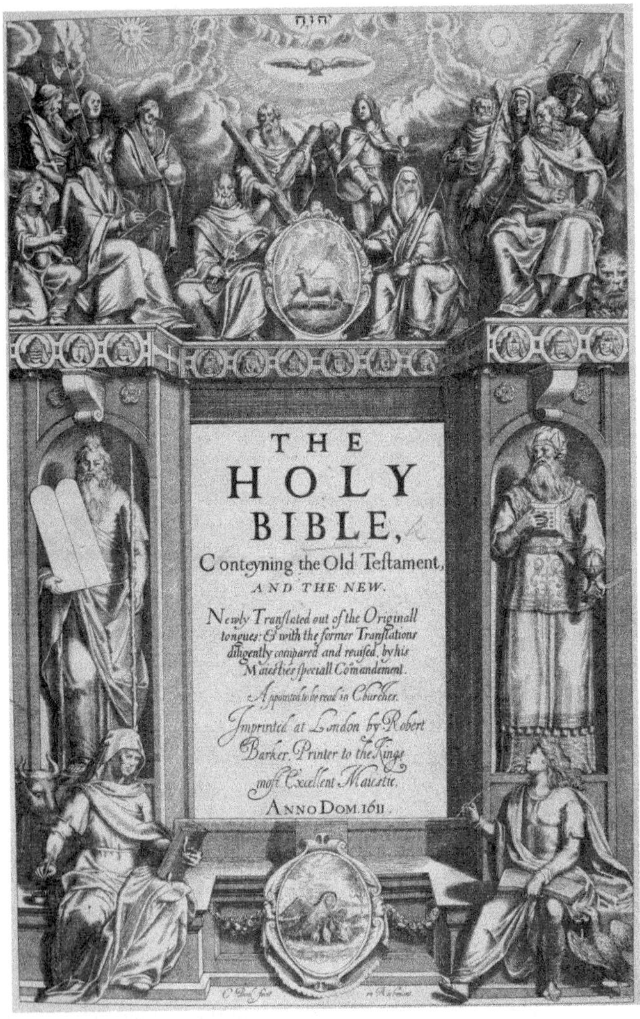

1. Title page from King James Bible.

guides (15:14). On the other hand, we must not overlook the obvious, which is that the evangelists were principally writing down a record of the life, death, and resurrection of Jesus. They were recording for posterity, and importantly giving their own view of, the events on which their faith was centred. They would hardly have undertaken such a labour simply for a small congregation in one particular settlement. Certainly such works quickly gained a wider circulation, and there were soon more in circulation than the four which we now know from the New Testament.

As the number of Christian writings in circulation in the churches scattered around the Mediterranean grew, so it became necessary to draw up an agreed list of authoritative texts which could be appealed to in matters of teaching and practice. The evidence for this process is scattered and often indirect. Scholars examine the use of the various Christian books by theologians during the period from the 2nd to the 5th centuries, as well as ecclesiastical rulings on the authority or orthodoxy of particular books.

The first stage in the formation of the canon was the making of collections of Christian writings. Paul's letters were the earliest writings to be collected, some time at the beginning of the 2nd century. The earliest collection has ten letters (1 and 2 Corinthians, Romans, Ephesians, 1 and 2 Thessalonians, Galatians, Philippians, Colossians, Philemon). Later versions add the so-called Pastoral Epistles: 1 and 2 Timothy and Titus. Eventually the Epistle to the Hebrews (which, unlike the others, does not contain an opening address by Paul to the recipients) was also added. By the end of the 2nd century the collection enjoyed widespread respect and use among church leaders, despite (or because of?) the fact that it had been the main source of doctrine of one of the earliest 'heretics', Marcion.

The next collection to emerge was the fourfold Gospel. This was more contentious. The four canonical Gospels were probably all written by the end of the 1st century, but that was by no means the end of the writing of Gospels. This overproduction of good news caused problems for the ordinary reader, who could easily be confused by such diversity in fundamental matters of the faith. In 170 Tatian unsuccessfully sought to find a solution by composing a single narrative out of Matthew, Mark, and Luke, with some additional oral material. By the end of the 2nd century a 'fourfold gospel' had come to be accepted. It contained four books, each of which told 'the' gospel according to the perspective of the particular evangelist. Such acceptance of diversity is remarkable, enshrining a political compromise at the heart of the Christian canon: no one contender, not even a hybrid, could command overwhelming support. Behind this compromise one might discern a wider perception that no one account could be adequate to express the one gospel to which all four witness. This understanding is reflected in the titles given to the Gospels: 'the Gospel according to Matthew', etc. The Gospels are to be seen as attempts, from their different standpoints, to express the mystery of what has been revealed to the Church.

While these two collections were fixed by the end of the 2nd century, there was less agreement about the contents of the third major section which would be included in the New Testament canon: the Catholic epistles. These were letters which were held to have been written to all the churches, rather than to a particular congregation. Generally, though not universally, 1 Peter and 1 John were accepted as canonical in the 2nd and 3rd centuries. Other writings took longer to be accepted: James, 2 Peter (a late work), 2 and 3 John (very polemical writings, *inter alia* forbidding believers even to greet those who are considered deviant to the group), and Jude had much less support. 2 and 3 John were still rejected in parts of the East as late as the 6th century.

It appears then that the process of acceptance of Christian writings by the churches was a gradual one, closely connected with the formation of such collections. In the 4th century a number of lists of canonical writings were made, which in differing measure contain much of what is in the present canon and a certain amount that is not. There are also significant variations, especially in regard to 2 Peter, 2 and 3 John, Hebrews, Jude, and Revelation, which are omitted from some lists.

This long process was eventually concluded by a series of decisions of church councils, though none of these councils was a general (ecumenical) council of the Church. Even so there was still disagreement. The Council of Laodicaea (363) omitted Revelation from the list; the Councils of Hippo (393) and Carthage (397) gave the present list of twenty-seven books. As a general rule, books were included which were judged to have been written by one of the apostles, to have been addressed to the Church at large (meeting the criterion of catholicity) and from the early times, and which were believed to be orthodox. These criteria were, however, applied flexibly: there were doubts about the apostolic authorship of Hebrews; the Pauline epistles were not strictly catholic; Jude and 2 Peter had not enjoyed a long tradition of use. Revelation was questioned, partly because it had been popular among heretical groups (such as the Montanists), partly because there were those who claimed that its promises would be fulfilled in an earthly reign of Christ, a view easily associated with political unrest and subversion. Its apostolic authorship was attacked and it was not accepted in the East until the 10th/11th centuries.

What's the use of a canon?

We have just had a very brief look at how different collections of books were made by different faith communities and had sacred and normative status conferred on them. We saw how, in both Jewish and Christian communities, this process was for the most part informal: different collections of books came to be recognized as sacred, authoritative, particularly appropriate for use in worship. To use the language of later Christian theology, the process of reception of the canon preceded that of formal definition. Moreover, this process of recognition was often a contentious one. It was not only a question of certain collections gradually gaining popularity. There were also books whose position within a collection, or within the final authorized collection, was contested. People wanted to fight not only for the inclusion but also for the exclusion of certain works. In the East the book of Revelation, with its millenarian fervour, was regarded with great suspicion. Such books were subversive and only to be treated with great caution and interpretative skill.

That is to say, the process of canonization of scripture is a process of conferring authority on some books and of refusing to confer authority on others. Sacred books carry a charge which has to be carefully controlled: they are a source of power and life for the communities which use them, but they are also potentially threatening. The communities which live by them may also grow apart by them. The same scriptures which have sustained a community through its history may suddenly be turned against it and cause painful and violent rifts.

What sort of authority is canonical authority as applied to writings? Moshe Halberthal, a Jewish philosopher teaching in Jerusalem, has helpfully distinguished different types of such authority: normative and formative. To recognize certain texts as canonical may be to declare that they contain (or generate) norms which regulate the lives of the communities which accept them. They provide the means for the community to make decisions, to manage conflicts, and to give rulings in matters of belief and practice. Law codes are perhaps the best example of such texts. Declaring the Bible to be canonical is on this view to declare that it can all be read as a source of rulings on faith and practice for the Church. Practices which are described in the Bible may then be regarded as prescribing (or at the least as permitting) certain forms of action: for example, prayers for the dead (2 Maccabees 12:43–4) or the extermination of indigenous peoples (Joshua, Judges, 1 Samuel 15).

Canonical writings may also have a formative use. Literary classics which form the basis of educational curricula in certain countries may have no normative, legal force, but they still have a very powerful formative role in the communities which accept them. The classical literature of ancient Greece, 'the Bible and Shakespeare', Goethe and Schiller, and other classics have variously provided communities in Europe and North America with a common language and thought which enables them to discourse about and to make sense of their experience. Communities shaped by such a body of writings will tend to share certain basic beliefs about the world and the proper ways to behave in this world, which will both strongly bond them together and also provide the means of conducting fierce internal debates about these common beliefs.

In practice, the biblical scriptures have exercised such a formative role, every bit as much as being drawn on as a source of rules and norms for the life and faith of the community. They have provided ordinary believers—and indeed those with no particularly strong beliefs—with tools to make sense of their lives, which they have done in many different ways. For many this has not been the stuff of controversy. Liturgies, hymns, prayers all take up scriptural phrases, images and metaphors, narratives and shape believers' attitudes, moods, and values.

On occasion these different uses of biblical language and imagery to make sense of experience have generated fierce debate and conflict. The Jews who lived at Qumran lived out of the same scriptures as other contemporary Jews; they shared with them basic beliefs about the Temple, the Land, the Law, and the covenant, but they disagreed strongly about the detailed interpretation of these beliefs. The Christian Reformers of the 16th century shared many of the same beliefs as the popes and priests of the Catholic Church. But they read scripture differently. When Luther finally grasped the sense of the expression 'the righteousness of God' on which he was to found the Reformation, he said that it was as if the gates of paradise had been opened to him: a whole new way of reading scripture, and therefore of conceiving the world and human action and behaviour, flowed from this breakthrough. This was then given powerful expression in popular tracts and in a flowering of hymnody, which shaped a whole new religious sensibility, very different from that of the medieval Church. The fact that 1st-century Jews and 16th-century Reformers and Catholics then appealed to scripture as normative, as a means of providing authoritative rulings in such debates, only aggravated the conflict.

The history of reception of the Bible gives ample examples of both these ways of reading a canonical text. There are sections of the Bible which easily lend themselves to a normative use, most obviously the law codes in Exodus and Leviticus and household codes in Colossians (3:18–4:1) and Ephesians (5:22–6:9), though attempting to put such rulings from a very different world into practice may cause many difficulties.

But such texts are the exception rather than the rule. Most texts do not easily lend themselves to such use. They are the product of a long process of composition and compilation. They are by no means always unambiguous. Many of the texts are metaphoric or poetic, intended to prompt people to re-envision their own world in their light, rather than simply to prescribe a way of looking at it. In all such cases the role of readers will not be simply to derive a set of rulings from them but to read them formatively, in such a way as to illuminate and shape their own beliefs and experience of the world.

Halberthal makes a further important point about the inclusion of a text within one's canon of scripture: it sets limits on, in a sense changes, the meaning of the text. The presumption now must be that if it is an authoritative text for this community, it must support and in some sense be suitable for regulating its beliefs and practice. But what if it is apparently at odds with the community's beliefs and expectations? The Song of Songs is a wonderful, and wonderfully explicit, love song: but what can be made of such a poem as sacred scripture? The outlook of the book of Ecclesiastes is profoundly sceptical: what is to be made of a book which appears to deny outright that there is any connection between virtue and vice and rewards and punishments? In such cases interpretative strategies may need to be found to reduce the dissonances and to bring harmony into the discord of the sacred writings. Their meaning, as Halberthal somewhat provocatively puts it, is changed by virtue of their inclusion in the canon of scripture. If they are here, then they must have an appropriate meaning.

Similar points could be made about the change in sense which occurs when texts like the Gospels and the Pauline letters become part of the Christian canon. Rulings, say about what women should wear on their head in church (1 Corinthians 11:5–6), which strongly echo cultural beliefs of the time and were part of specific rulings to settle arguments within particular 1st-century Christian communities, come to assume the status of eternal divine law. The Gospels which had been regarded as the reminiscences of the apostles, whose principal function was to provide sources for Jesus's sayings and deeds, come to be regarded as authoritative interpretations of the meanings of those sayings and deeds.

In the second half of this book we will look more closely at a variety of readings of the biblical texts, mostly by believers, but also by those outside the various faith communities which have lived out of the Bible. This will be in large measure a descriptive exercise: I hope that the sheer variety of readings associated with these texts will provoke a certain respect. For some, such respect will be coupled with affection, even love. For others, it may be more like the respect one accords to an unexploded bomb. It is not hard to see why such different reactions are both possible and appropriate.

Before we do that, however, we need to consider how this collection of books was given a variety of linguistic and physical forms, and distributed across the world.

Chapter 4
Translation, production, and distribution of the Bible

The previous two chapters have shown the complexity of the process by which a number of closely related but distinct Bibles, collections of books taken from a wider pool of writings, were adopted by Jewish and Christian communities as their authoritative texts. A long history ran from, say, the utterances of an 8th-century prophet, Isaiah, to the inclusion of a 65-chapter-long work in the list of authoritative texts which made up the Jewish or the Christian canon.

There is a further story to be told. How did/do the adherents of those religious communities, or, indeed, does anyone at all, get access to those texts? For centuries Isaiah's prophecies would have been preserved in Hebrew on scrolls, read aloud at gatherings of the different communities which acknowledged their authority, available to the religious professionals for private study and reflection. Later, at the turn of the first millennium CE with the introduction of the codex (essentially a forerunner of the book), this will have changed and some at least of the Bible will have become more readily available to those who could read. By the 4th century CE, the whole of the Bible would be found in codex form.

As we have seen, too, language could be an obstacle. By the 2nd century BCE there was a need for translations of the Hebrew scriptures into Greek. Latin translations of both Hebrew and

Greek originals and translations followed in the Roman period, and by the Middle Ages in the Christian West, the Bible was most readily available in Latin, and largely inaccessible to the majority of the population. Expense, education, and hierarchical control will have restricted direct access to the Bible largely to the clerisy, the trained professionals. Manuscripts, hand copies, were expensive. Literacy was largely restricted to the wealthy and the professionals. Only they could understand Latin, in the West the most common language in which the Bible was to be found. And, most importantly, if a collection as disparate in content, genre, and origin as this were to fulfil its intended role as arbiter of doctrine and morals for these communities, it required a professional body which could give a coherent and consistent view of its meaning.

But change was coming in the Christian West. The 15th century saw the growth of lay movements based on private prayer and, increasingly, Bible reading. It also saw the development of printing using movable type, which made possible the production of cheaper bibles. This prepared the way for the Protestant Reformation with its powerful desire to make the Bible available to all. It mounted a sustained attack on the authority of the papacy and its clergy; the process of translation, production, and distribution of bibles accelerated; there was a growth in educational opportunities for all, driven in large measure by the desire to make the scriptures available to a wider public; and there began an extraordinary effort to ensure that the majority of people in the world would have direct access to at least parts of the Bible.

We shall have more to say about the theological beliefs which lay at the heart of the Reformation but here it is important to catch at least some of the passion and urgency which drove this movement. Deep anxieties about the fate which awaited them after death plagued men and women in the late medieval period. One only has to look at the many pictures of the Last Judgement which adorn churches of the period to understand some of this. Luther certainly was plagued by fears of eternal punishment and torment. In his anxiety he turned to and found release from these fears through his reading of Paul's letters. This became for him the gateway to Paradise.

The Protestant Reformation was thus based on an intensely personal experience of reading scripture. This was not without precedent. Medieval theologians, like Thomas Aquinas, based their work on the reading of sacred scripture. That experience of reading scripture for oneself was extended to a wider, lay public with the introduction of printed bibles in the 15th century. It was, as Diarmaid MacCulloch has pointed out, a solo activity, which in itself encouraged 'more inward-looking, personalized' forms of devotion. Now the Reformers sought to make such experience available to all who looked for release from deep fears of judgement. The liberation this brought struck a deep chord in many of the major cities of late medieval Europe, enabling them to throw off papal control. Here, in the reading of the Bible, was an authority which overrode all others, even that of the papacy and the princes.

How was such an experience to be shared more widely? The first task was to make the text of the Bible more widely available in the vernacular. Under John Wycliffe in the 14th century the Bible had been translated into Middle English and circulated in manuscript form. Printed translations from the Latin into the vernacular had appeared in High and Low German, Italian, Dutch, Spanish, Czech, and Catalan by the end of the 15th century. Luther began his translation of the Bible from the Hebrew and Greek into German in 1521 while in hiding in the Wartburg and finally completed it in 1532. It opened the flood gates and translations, both Protestant and Catholic, began to appear across Europe. In England, Tyndale (1494–1536) had pioneered the work which led to publication of the King James Version in 1611.

The scholarly effort required is not to be underestimated: Luther needed to acquire Hebrew and Greek, which had not been taught in the medieval Schools. Such translations had, too, enormous cultural significance. Luther's translation shapes the German language as the somewhat later King James Version, alongside Shakespeare, shapes the English language. Such works underlay the very way that people thought about and understood their world.

While the new translations undoubtedly had a deep impact on the European cultures into which they were made, their languages were already in a measure shaped by the beliefs and narratives of the Bible. A quite different situation arose in the 18th century. By then the Bible had been translated into most major European languages. A new wave of translations began as Christian missionaries extended their work into Africa and Asia. The first complete Bibles to be published in translation were into Tamil (1727) by Bartholomäus Ziegenbalg from Germany; and into Malay (1733) by the Dutchmen Melchior Leydekker and Peter van der Vorm. By 2001, according to the United Bible Society's Report, at least sections of the Bible had been translated into 2,287 languages worldwide, of which only 203 were European. The sheer size of this undertaking is extraordinary.

The amount of ethnographic, philological, and lexicographical work which made that possible is hard to imagine. In many cases, such work led to the documentation and indeed revivifying of local languages. In 1999, many thousands of Baptists gathered in Chin State, Burma, to celebrate the 100th anniversary of the arrival of Baptist missionaries. Asked how they had managed to get permission from the—very anti-Christian—Burmese government, they replied: 'We said we were celebrating the 100th anniversary of the writing-down of the Chin language.'

Lamin Sanneh has documented some of the early attempts by missionary translators to find appropriate words for God and the ways in which this led them to explore local beliefs and customs. He describes an early encounter in the 1730s between George

Schmidt, a Moravian missionary, and the Khoikhoi people he had come to bring out of darkness. When he told them why he had come, they replied:

'That is good, *baas* [master].'
I asked them, Schmidt says, if they knew that there was a great Baas, who had given them their cattle and all they possessed.
'Yes, replied the tribesmen.'
'What do you call him?'
'We call him Tui-qua,' was the reply.

This was the beginning of a new relationship between Schmidt and the Khoikhoi: as he embraced their language and terms for God, he entered more closely into their cultural milieu. The God whom he had come to tell them about was also the God whom he needed to learn more about from them. Similarly, the Bible that he was bringing was about to be refashioned. The Bible that would subsequently appear in translation was not simply a foreign implant but itself a rereading of the Bible, reshaping it with concepts and names from the indigenous cultures. And at the same time, Sanneh insists, those cultures would be transformed and enlivened, as was German and English culture by the great translations of the 16th and 17th centuries.

Bible production

As we have seen, the physical form of written works has constantly changed through history: engravings on stone, cuneiform impressions on clay tablets, scrolls, codices, printed books, e-books, audio books, and more. The Reformation was preceded by a major development in the production of written works: the printing press using movable type of Gutenberg (1437) and Caxton (1476). Wooden or metal type could be set a few pages at a time and this would allow the production of some 200–250 pages an hour. It was a technology that lent itself more to the production of short books and pamphlets than huge works like the Bible and the

Reformation was probably spread more by 'Flugschriften' (tracts) than by the distribution of copies of the Bible in the vernacular. Bible production grew through the 16th and 17th centuries. Larger copies would go to churches, colleges, and the clergy and gentry; smaller copies were used in schools and given to parishioners and to children.

A further, major advance in private Bible reading began in the 18th century, driven by the renewal movements: Pietism in Germany and the revivalist movement stemming from the Wesleys in England and then spreading to North America. This was only possible through the production of bibles in numbers and at a cost previously difficult to achieve. Till then most bibles had been printed in small houses with only enough type to set a few pages at a time, before being broken up and reset. This was slow and could lead to errors in typesetting in any subsequent edition, a matter of major concern to church authorities.

Then in 1710 Baron Karl Hildebrand von Cannstein founded the Cannstein Bible Institute at Halle. He could afford to invest in sufficient type to keep the whole text of the Luther Bible 'standing', ready for reprinting and for any corrections which needed to be made. Between 1710 and 1719 when Cannstein died, the Institute produced 100,000 copies of the New Testament and 40,000 bibles.

Yet the real breakthrough, which would allow the production of bibles on an industrial scale, came only at the beginning of the 19th century. Three major changes occurred. First, steam power was used to make paper. The Foudrinier machine (1804) produced paper not in individual sheets but in continuous rolls. Second, the technology of stereotype was introduced. Once pages were set in type, moulds were made from plaster of Paris or papier maché and stereotype plates cast using an alloy of tin, antimony, and lead. The type used could then be broken up and used again. And, importantly, the moulds could be corrected without having to reset the type. Third, significant improvements would be made in book-binding to meet the demands of the Bible societies who provided and developed the markets for the books.

Books now became available to people of all classes and the publishing world was transformed. Large numbers of cheap bibles could be produced. Religious publishing houses were quick to exploit this opportunity. By the middle of the 19th century the American Methodist Book Concern in New York had grown into the largest publishing house of any kind in the world.

There remained the question of distribution of bibles. Here the Bible Societies were to play a crucial role. Bibles at this date were being distributed in limited numbers by the Society for Promoting Christian Knowledge. At a Religious Tract Society (RTS) meeting in 1804, a Welsh Calvinist Methodist minister, Thomas Charles of Bala, told the story of Mary Jones, a young Welsh girl who had saved up money to buy a Welsh-language bible from her earnings, and had walked miles to buy it only to find that supplies had run out. Those present at the meeting decided on the spot to found a new society, to be known as the British and Foreign Bible Society (BFBS), to distribute affordable editions of the scriptures not only in England and Wales but—for good measure—across the whole British Empire and the rest of the world.

The society was ecumenical, principally made up of Evangelicals of different theological persuasions. In order to avoid internal doctrinal conflict, bibles were to be distributed 'without note or comment'. A central administration was established at Bible House in London but the driving force lay in local associations, particularly the Ladies Associations, responsible for raising funds for local and overseas distribution. In what was regarded as a providential conjunction, the development of the BFBS coincided not only with the developments in book production already described but also with the growth in urban populations and the work of the RTS and the growing Sunday School movement to provide reading and writing skills to the children of the poor. The potential market for religious literature and for bibles in particular was enormous.

Similar developments followed in North America. The American Bible Society (ABS) was founded in 1816 in Philadelphia by a number of local societies. It had similarly ambitious aims to those of the BFBS. In 1829, it decided to put a bible into every household within the United States within two years.

Both the BFBS and the ABS had foreign ambitions and links with other Bible societies. The BFBS had a Foreign Secretary, Karl Friedrich August Steinkopf. When the Napoleonic Wars ended in 1815, he developed a system of colporteurs, door-to-door salesmen, who travelled across Europe selling bibles. Their stories of heroism and endurance as they met opposition, particularly in Catholic lands, were the stuff of society publications, and George Borrow's *The Bible in Spain* (1843) achieved the status of a minor classic. It contained, among much else, vivid descriptions of Roma people which caught the attention of Prosper Mérimée, the author of the novella *Carmen* on which Bizet's opera is based.

Not all such ventures were met with opposition. The first BFBS bibles in Spanish had already reached Buenos Aires and Montevideo by 1806, only two years after the society's foundation. By 1807, the BFBS had printed 20,000 copies in Portuguese which sailors distributed along the coast of Brazil. A major development occurred with the arrival of James (Diego) Thompson at the River Plate in 1818. He was both a colporteur and an educationalist promoting literacy through the Lancaster method.

Joseph Lancaster had founded a school in Southwark, a poor area of London, in 1798. Relying on monitors, more advanced students who helped with teaching the younger pupils, he was able to enrol more than 1,000 children at a time. This method, and its success, attracted much attention among those who sought to promote revolutionary democratic ideals, including leaders in Latin America. Lancaster was invited to Venezuela by Simon Bolívar and also worked in Colombia.

Thompson was similarly welcomed by liberal movements further south, in Argentina, Chile, Peru, and Montevideo, in all of which countries he founded schools. Thompson taught his pupils to practise their reading skills on selections from the Bible. For a while, he had total freedom in choosing such excerpts. In 1826, the BFBS engaged him to work in Ecuador, Mexico, and the Caribbean. Within a short period, bibles were being distributed in twenty-five countries. However, reaction against Thompson's activities was not long coming. The Spanish king Fernando VII drew closer to the Vatican and from 1830 onwards edicts were issued prohibiting the distribution of bibles in Spanish and without notes. Thousands of bibles were removed from bookshops or seized at ports. Not all was bad and work progressed in the Caribbean and Venezuela. The BFBS raised funds to provide every emancipated slave with a copy of the Bible to 'help console him and the wrongs he had suffered'. Thompson was present at the emancipation of black slaves in Jamaica on 1 August 1834.

What is remarkable about this story and indeed the story of Bible distribution across Europe, Africa, and Asia is the sheer energy and expansiveness of the work. Over time, the methods of distribution change; cooperation between the larger Bible societies grows; the process becomes indigenized, with local churches and societies playing a greater role. Sometimes the societies would find themselves working with strange bedfellows. The advent of a communist government in China in 1949 effectively closed down the operations of the Bible societies and placed them in the hands of local Chinese. While some chose to import bibles illegally into China, the majority eventually agreed with the Chinese government to establish a press operated by the Amity Foundation, an independent organization set up by the local state-sanctioned churches. Over $8 million was raised by different societies and by 2000, thirteen years later, Amity had printed 25 million bibles.

One way or another, with very different agencies, the work of Bible distribution over two centuries had wrought extraordinary cultural change. A movement initially driven and financed by local associations of evangelical Christians, strongly supported in terms of sales and of fundraising by Ladies Associations, had brought about the spread of the Bible into all parts of the world. In the process the Bible had changed too. Not only had the formats in which it was distributed multiplied but so too, even more, had the languages in which it appeared. Partly through the process of translation, partly through its reading by people with very different world-views and beliefs, it had become embedded in local, traditional cultures, transforming and renewing those cultures, as it in turn became integrated into them. It is certainly true that Western commerce and colonialism would provide the context and many of the opportunities for this spread, and would seek support from the Bible for its activities. But in the end the indigenization of the Bible meant that it was not simply seen as the colonists' book. Among the colonized and enslaved, there were those who saw in it a book which could ultimately empower them in their search for freedom, in which they could find hope and consolation and which they wanted to retain—as theirs—when the colonizers left.

Chapter 5
Jewish and Christian readings of the Binding of Isaac

Texts, once canonized, undergo change. They become sacred texts. In the communities which recognize their new status, believers regard them as set apart, special texts to be treated like no other texts. Their expectations about these texts are very different from those they have of other texts. As sacred texts, it is unthinkable that they should conflict with believers' own deepest sense of the sacred. Any serious dissonance between the community's experience and the world of the sacred text cries out for resolution. Either the world of the text must be made to conform to the experience of the community, or the community must change to conform with the text. A powerful dialectic is set up. Believers read the texts in the light of their own experience; and, at the same time, they look to the texts to make sense of and to shape that experience. Different communities of believers will read the same text in very different ways. In this we will find a reflection both of their different beliefs and their different histories.

This is not altogether different from what happens with classical, non-sacred texts, but the intensity of the reactions is different. Gustave Flaubert was tried for obscenity after the serialization of *Madame Bovary*. After his acquittal the novel was published in book form and became a best-seller, still regarded as his greatest work. The comparison is instructive: such conflicts between literary and aesthetic works and respectable taste and sensibilities

Box 3

Regardless of the persuasiveness of this or any particular interpretation, that conviction lies at the heart of Midrash all the time: the Scriptures are not only a record of the past but a prophecy, a foreshadowing and foretelling, of what will come to pass. And if that is the case, text and personal experience are not two autonomous domains. On the contrary, they are reciprocally enlightening: even as the immediate event helps make the age-old sacred text intelligible, so in turn the text reveals the fundamental significance of the recent event or experience.

Judah Goldin

mostly create only a temporary scandal; they rarely lead to lasting divisions in a community. They may well lead to changes in sensibility. Writers and artists enable people to come to terms with the heights and depths of experience which polite society simply ignores or suppresses. Changes in sensibility also occur, as we shall see, in religious communities as they engage with new texts or readings of texts. Such encounters often generate much greater resistance, as communities fight to defend ways of looking at the world which are sanctified by inherited readings of scripture (Box 3).

Let us now consider a single text which has had profound resonances in both the Jewish and Christian traditions and look at some of the ways in which it has shaped and been shaped by the very different experiences of these two families of communities.

The Akedah

The Akedah, the story of Abraham's binding of Isaac in Genesis 22, touches a deep nerve in Jewish and Christian sensibilities. It is a story of strange violence and tenderness, of a father ordered by his God to sacrifice 'his only son'. Only at the last moment are Abraham and Isaac rescued from the approaching horror by the intervention of an angel. The story is told with all the power and economy and concreteness of biblical narrative at its best. Abraham and Isaac leave the servants behind and set off: 'Abraham took the wood of the burnt offering and laid it on his son Isaac; and he himself carried the fire and the knife. So the two of them walked on together' (Genesis 22:6). That last sentence, repeated two verses later, and the ensuing short dialogue emphasize the bonds between the two and their fear and dread; yet Abraham's obedience to God drives them on to the mountain of sacrifice. There he stretches out his hand and takes up the knife to kill his son. Only then does the angel intervene. Out of the near disaster comes the renewal of the promise of a new nation springing from the father and his son.

The range of emotions and experiences which is embraced in this short, tersely written narrative is remarkable, and this is reflected in the richness of its subsequent readings.

One of the earliest interpretations of the story is found in the book of Jubilees. Its origin in the 2nd century BCE suggests that the writer is reflecting on the terrible events of the proscription of Judaism by the Seleucid king Antiochus Epiphanes. In form, it is a retelling of Genesis and the early chapters of Exodus. The major section of the work is narrated to Moses by the angel of the presence. This enables the writer to fill in the heavenly background to the story, explaining why it was that God tested Abraham (Genesis 22:1). Reports circulating in heaven about Abraham's faithfulness and love of God had prompted Satan to challenge the genuineness of Abraham's love for God, asserting that Abraham loved his son Isaac more. God, knowing that Abraham's love was genuine, for he had already tested him many times, nevertheless prepares one final trial for Abraham. This theme of the last trial will run on through Jewish discussions of the story.

Thus in Jubilees the motif of Abraham's trial in Genesis receives a subtle yet significant shift of emphasis. The trial is no longer a means for God to find out whether Abraham loves and obeys him. God (and the reader) knows this from the start, and at the crucial moment God intervenes because of this knowledge. In Genesis, once Abraham has taken the knife God, through the angel, can say, 'for now I know that you fear God, since you have not withheld your son, your only son, from me' (Genesis 22:12). In Jubilees the purpose of God's action is to demonstrate publicly what God already knew: Abraham's faithfulness and love of God. 'And I have made known to all that you are faithful to me in everything which I say to you.' This then becomes a message to the Jews in times of persecution. The purpose of Abraham's and, by extension, their own trials is to make Israel's faithfulness to God known, so that 'all the nations may bless themselves' by them (Jubilees 18:16).

The introduction of Satan adds a further dimension to the story, alongside the motif of God's testing of Abraham's obedience. The world contains dark powers who wish to claim even the most righteous as their victims. In a rather obscure way, some of the responsibility for human suffering falls upon Satan, while God and his angels are portrayed as being there to support and protect the faithful, ensuring that no harm comes to Isaac (at least no physical harm). But how does this chime in with Jewish experiences down the ages of persecution and martyrdom?

Such problems trouble the 1st-century Jewish writer Philo of Alexandria. The prosperous and educated Jewish community in Alexandria also suffered discrimination and persecution. In his treatise *De Abrahamo*, he deals first with accusations that Abraham's trial was of no great account compared with those pagans who had willingly sacrificed offspring for the preservation of their cities or people. But, says Philo, for Abraham, for whom human sacrifice was abominable, sacrificing his son would have been an even more terrible trial. For pagan princes, such a thing would have been almost second nature (*De Abrahamo*, 177–99). Philo reflects more widely on human suffering and affliction, drawing out the allegorical significance of the story. Isaac's name means laughter. Abraham sacrifices laughter, or rather 'the good emotion of the understanding, that is joy', out of a sense of duty to God. This is proper because a life of pure joy and happiness is for God alone. Nevertheless, God will allow those who are faithful to share a measure of such joy, though even so it will be admixed with sorrow (*De Abrahamo*, 200–7). One is reminded of the Jewish joke: Why don't Jews get drunk? Because when you drink, you forget your troubles.

But what of the greater sufferings of Jews themselves? The terrible persecution inflicted on Jews at the time of Antiochus Epiphanes (175 BCE) produced its own tales of Jewish faithfulness to God under extreme torture. One of these (in 2 Maccabees 7) tells of a mother who witnesses—and encourages—the gruesome martyrdom of her seven sons, before she herself too is killed. In a later rabbinic retelling, the story is transposed from its original setting in the time of Antiochus Epiphanes to the 2nd century CE, when Jews were persecuted under the Roman emperor Hadrian. The story is full both of the pain of such suffering and of Jewish pride in their martyrs. 'The mother wept and said [to her sons]: Children, do not be distressed, for to this end were you created—to sanctify in the world the Name of the Holy One, blessed be He. Go and tell Father Abraham: Let not your heart swell with pride! You built one altar, but I have built seven altars and on them have offered up my seven sons. What is more: Yours was a trial; mine was an accomplished fact!' (Yalkut, Deuteronomy 26, 938).

An even more anguished response to the story comes in the medieval retellings during the persecutions of the Jews in the Rhineland at the time of the Crusades. The Jewish chronicles of the time record how, when the Crusaders attacked, Jews, rather than risk forced conversion under torture, would offer each other up as a sacrifice, inspecting the knife for blemishes that might render the sacrifice invalid, and reciting an appropriate blessing.

The synagogue poetry of the time compares such sacrifices with the Akedah of Isaac:

> O Lord, Mighty One, dwelling on high!
> Once, over one Akedah, Ariels cried out before Thee,
> But now how many are butchered and burned!
> Why over the blood of children did they not raise a cry?
> Before that patriarch could in his haste sacrifice his only one,
> It was heard from heaven: Do not put forth your hand to destroy!
> But how many sons and daughters of Judah are slain—
> While yet He makes no haste to save those butchered nor those cast on the flames.
>
> *Fragment from a Threnody* by R. Eliezer bar Joel ha-Levi

But the most remarkable treatment of the Akedah story from this period comes from R. Ephraim ben Jacob of Bonn. Here we read that Abraham not only actually carried out the ritual slaughter of his son, but that, when God immediately brought Isaac back to life, he attempted to repeat the sacrifice.

> He [Abraham] made haste, he pinned him [Isaac] down with his knees,
> He made his two arms strong,
> With steady hands he slaughtered him according to the rite,
> Full right was the slaughter.
> Down upon him fell the resurrecting dew, and he revived. (The father) seized him (then) to slaughter him once more.
> Scripture bear witness! Well-grounded is the fact:
> And the Lord called Abraham, even a second time from heaven.

Remarkably the poet claims scriptural support for his account of Abraham's attempt to sacrifice his son a second time. In the Genesis story, it is true, the angel calls Abraham twice, once to stop the sacrifice, once to give Abraham the promise that he will be the father of a great nation. R. Ephraim gives a very different rendering of the two calls. Abraham evidently fails to hear, or ignores, the first. Spiegel, in his deeply sympathetic account of this poem, comments tersely on the phrase 'well-grounded is the fact': 'if not in Scripture, then in the experience of the Jews in the Middle Ages' (p. 138). The terrible experiences of Jews in the persecutions of the Middle Ages must find an echo in their sacred texts.

Christian interpretation of the Akedah, by contrast, is refracted through its own central narrative of the crucifixion of Jesus. When Jesus prays to God in the Garden of Gethsemane on the night before his crucifixion, we may hear distant echoes of Isaac's questioning of his father and the subsequent traditions of his willing acceptance of his father's purpose. Certainly, the plot is different: there is no human father as mediator of God's purposes; no relenting on the part of the heavenly father; no mere testing of the victim's father. Rather it is the victim himself who must struggle to accept freely the heavenly Father's unwavering will (a motif which does indeed occur in some of the versions of the Akedah). In Mark's account, Jesus prays: 'Abba, Father, for you all things are possible; remove this cup from me; yet not what I want, but what you want' (Mark 14:36). Matthew and Luke seem to stumble over Mark's bald 'for you all things are possible', a traditional ascription of omnipotence. Matthew, faced with the enormity of God's killing his own son, seems to raise the question whether there is not some higher necessity controlling the action: 'Father, if it is possible, let this cup pass from me' (Matthew 26:39). Luke seems more concerned with the question of the unity or constancy of the divine will: how can the Son of God pray to God in order to change his mind? Jesus prays: 'Father if you are willing' (Luke 22:42). John omits the whole episode of Jesus's prayer in the garden, replacing it with a comparable scene of anguish immediately before the Last Supper (12:27). He makes this a more public scene at which not only Jews but Greeks are present. Jesus's acceptance of his mission will glorify the divine name, just as Abraham's obedience had done before.

Only at one point is this emphasis on the relentlessness of the Father's will qualified: in the evangelists' vivid portrayal of the human actors who conspire to bring about Jesus's death. Mark's account of Jesus's arrest is introduced by Jesus's own words: 'Enough; the hour has come; the Son of Man is delivered into the hands of sinners. Rise, let us be going; see, he who will deliver me is at hand' (Mark 14:41–2). There is an ambiguity here in the Greek word for 'deliver'. It means both simply 'hand over' and also 'betray'. Does it refer to Judas's betraying him to the chief priests? Or does it not also suggest the divine agency behind the events which now overwhelm Jesus, handing him over into the hands of his destroyers? (The same—Greek—word occurs in Isaiah 53:6: 'the Lord has delivered on to [laid on] him our transgressions'.) Probably both senses are to be understood, but the ensuing narrative, with its repeated use of the verb 'seize' and references to the mob's 'swords and clubs', emphasizes the violent action of the mob. Jesus is caught up in the chief priests' and scribes' plans to kill him and they, after a perfunctory trial, 'bind him' and 'deliver' him to Pilate.

It is tempting to see here an inversion of the themes in the Genesis narrative. There Abraham takes Isaac, binds him, and offers him up to God in obedience to God's command. Here it is sinners who seize Jesus and bind him and hand him over to the foreign tyrant for execution. Yet in both cases, as the scene in Gethsemane has made clear, it is God who wills these events. In the one case, Abraham's last trial prepares him to be the father of a multitude of nations in accordance with God's promise to him (Genesis 17:4); he is to be the type of ethical monotheism, of radical obedience to the will of God. In the other, Jesus is singled out as the instrument of God's will in the conflict with human wickedness. The sacrifice of Jesus is not so much the test of obedience (though it is that too) as the point of engagement between the divine agent and the forces of destruction and death in the world. It is the point of transition from the world of violence and death to the new age of life, which is anticipated in Jesus's resurrection.

Subsequent Christian retellings of the story of Jesus's Passion repeat this pattern of indirect allusion and variation. In John's

Passion narrative Jesus (not Simon of Cyrene as in the other Gospels) 'goes out, bearing his cross, to the place called the place of the skull' (19:17). Like Isaac, Jesus bears the means of his death. This, intriguingly, is mirrored in rabbinic retellings of the Isaac story, which say that Isaac bears the wood like one who bears his cross. Christian exegesis links this motif to Christian experience of suffering. Christian willingness to bear suffering is seen as continuous with Abraham's faith: 'Righteously also do we, possessing the same faith as Abraham, and taking up the cross as Isaac did the wood, follow Him' (Irenaeus, *Against Heresies*, IV.5.4). Later piety has elaborated this motif in the Stations of the Cross, which line the walls of Catholic churches and depict Jesus falling three times under the weight of the cross. Mantegna's painting of Abraham and Isaac places greater emphasis on the sacrifice itself, contrasting the imminent sacrifice of the bound Isaac with the lamb, not caught in a thicket, but climbing willingly on to the rather stylized altar, ready for slaughter. Lest we should miss the reference to Jesus as the sacrificial lamb, the altar is shaded by a fruit-bearing tree, a clear reminder of the sin which will be expiated by the coming sacrifice.

However, in Christian interpretation the Isaac story is not always directly related to Christ's death. Rembrandt in his etching (see Figure 2) has the angel not merely calling out to Abraham but actively restraining him by putting his arms around him. The story has become a depiction of divine protection, symbolized by the tender care of the guardian angel—a far step from the medieval rabbis who read this through their experiences of persecution and genocide.

By contrast the Danish philosopher Kierkegaard again celebrates in Abraham the man of faith. He calls Abraham's willingness to sacrifice his son the 'teleological suspension of the ethical'. In religious faith normal ethical laws and rules are suspended, as men and women embrace overriding goals or ends. The true 'knight of faith' is one who moves beyond the world of ethics and

2. Rembrandt's etching of Abraham and Isaac, 1655. The angel's arms are round both Abraham and Isaac and its wings fill the picture. Isaac is unbound and offers himself willingly; Abraham appears to be bemused, almost in despair.

enters a world which is governed by divinely given commands and promises. Abraham's greatness lies in his continued trust and faith in God against all the odds: it was not just a faith in the afterlife, in some final resolution of things, but in the here and now, a belief that God's promises would be made good, even after the apparent impossibility of Sarah's conceiving a child, in the face of God's command to sacrifice him. Kierkegaard's writings are part of a profound and personally costly protest against a bourgeois normalization of Christianity. His suspension of 'normal' ethical standards remains dangerous and disturbing and brings out something of the strangeness and provocative nature of the original story, with its witness to a prodigious faith. If Abraham had not had faith, says Kierkegaard, he might heroically have sacrificed himself instead of Isaac. 'He would have been admired in the world, and his name would never be forgotten; but it is one thing to be admired and another to become a guiding star that saves the anguished.'

The rich afterlife of the biblical texts

The history of the reception of the biblical texts provides an almost inexhaustible fund of evidence of the vitality of these ancient writings. They have been read by very different faith communities in widely different circumstances and have generated readings of remarkable divergence as well as remarkable convergence. Explanations for this kind of fruitfulness are not easy to provide.

Part of the reason must lie in the diversity of contexts in which such texts are read; it is not surprising that the story of Isaac's binding will resonate differently with those under attack from marauding Crusaders than with those who, say, have to face the rigours of life in a mountain village in Catholic Austria. There is also a major difference in the literary context of the Isaac story as it is read by Jews and Christians. For Christians, with the massive concentration on the cross of Jesus in the New Testament writings, it is inevitable that the themes of the Akedah should be subsumed in their reading of the Passion. Isaac, as in the Mantegna painting, becomes the 'type of the one who was to come' (*Epistle of Barnabas* 7:3) and the various motifs of the story are taken up and used, sometimes by way of contrast, in the narrative and discursive development of the Passion. For Jews there is more cause to reflect on the meaning of the story in the light of the history of Abraham's descendants.

But diversity of context will not explain all: there is in the texts themselves a richness and an ambiguity which invites diversity of interpretation. Images like Abraham's stretching out his hand, or his laying the wood on his son, strike profound chords in later writers and interpreters. The richness of imagery and metaphor in the biblical writings, in its narrative, poetry, and more discursive writing, is such that it is bound to lead to readings which draw freely on the experience of the readers. Here are stories and texts which widely diverse communities have been able to make their own, precisely because of their evocative nature.

Chapter 6
Galatians through history

Paul's letter to the Galatians is one of the shorter works in the Bible and yet it has made a disproportionately deep impact on its readers and their communities down the ages. At the turn of the 4th century, it helped shape the new worlds which would emerge as the Roman Empire embraced Christianity. At the Reformation, it was one of the central texts for Luther. Its radical statements of human equality and renewal continue to resonate. This chapter will try to give a sense of the mark that this small book has left on 2,000 years of global history.

Galatians starts life, not as a sacred book, but as one contribution to a fierce debate about the meaning and application of sacred texts. Did the legal texts in the Hebrew scriptures mean that not only Jewish believers in Christ, like Peter and Paul, but also Gentile believers should observe Jewish food laws, even that they should be circumcised? As Chapter 2 relates, Paul had fallen out with Peter over this issue. He now has to show how the scriptures encompass the experience of liberation and release that Jewish and Gentile believers alike are enjoying, *whether or not they are law-observant*. In the course of doing that, he will also have to set out his newly acquired central convictions and begin to lay the foundations of the new way of life 'in the Spirit' which Christian believers, Jew or Gentile, are to follow. Within a few centuries this letter will become an authoritative text for Christians containing both some very prescriptive rulings and some equally evocative and suggestive accounts of the spiritual life.

We will look first at the way Paul deals with the central issue of Law observance and then try to give some idea of how later interpreters of his letter used his ideas and images to shape the life of the churches in their very different situations.

Paul's argument in Galatians

The letter falls into three sections. The first two chapters identify the issue: do believers in Christ need to obey the Law? and set out Paul's claims to speak on the matter with authority.

Chapters 3 and 4 then provide an alternative reading of the scriptures to his opponents' but not before Paul has reminded the Galatians of the new life in the Spirit which they received. This was not because they were particularly law observant, but because they believed (what Paul had preached to them) (3:1–5). The heart of the scriptures, Paul asserts in justification of this claim, is to be found not in the giving of the Law but in God's promise to Abraham. God blesses, rewards Abraham, not for his obedience to a Law which came 430 years later, but for his belief and trust in God. Abraham believed God's promise that he, though old and with an old wife, would be the father of a great nation. The Galatians too, because of their belief, share in that promise and, as Abraham's spiritual descendants, receive the blessing (3:1–9).

At this point, the argument becomes very dense. Paul needs to explain why God introduced the Law; why it was only temporary and indeed oppressive; and also why the fulfilment of the promise to Abraham was delayed. His key move is to argue that the promise was made to Abraham 'and his offspring' (Genesis 13:15; 17:8; 24:7). With keen attention to the precise wording of the scriptures, he points out that the word for offspring is in the singular and that it refers, therefore, not to all the physical offspring of Abraham but to 'one person, who is Christ' (3:16). This assertion, that the offspring to whom the promise was made was Christ, changes the whole perspective from which the scriptures are read. They are no longer seen through the eyes of a law-observant Jew, but through those of anyone, Jew or Gentile, who has come to find life through belief in Christ.

The Law now appears as a temporary holding measure to deal with sin in the world until Christ should come (3:19). It kept the Jews 'imprisoned and guarded… until faith would be revealed…was our disciplinarian until Christ came, so that we might be justified by faith' (3:23–4). It worked, that is to say, as a restraint, a protection, a severe guide. For those who live under it, it is a curse from which they need to be redeemed (3:10). When Christ comes, the promise is fulfilled and those who believe—and are baptized into Christ—are all 'children of God through faith'. Old distinctions between Jew and Greek, slave and free, indeed between male and female, are set aside as the world is made new (3:24–9).

In the final section (5–6), Paul explores the nature of the new life in Christ. How are those liberated from the Law to lead their lives, if they no longer have a legal code to live by? United with Christ and freed from the Law, they are now led by the Spirit. They bear the fruit of the Spirit in their lives. As they share each other's burdens, they fulfil the 'law' of Christ (6:2).

All this marks a radical break with the kind of Pharisaic Judaism that Paul had previously embraced. It was emerging as one of the dominant forms of Judaism which would find its full expression in the rabbinic Judaism which flowered over the following centuries. Here Paul asserts that such forms of law observance have no further relevance for those who believe in Christ (Gal. 6:15). And that Christian believers who assert the contrary are anathema, accursed (1:9).

The reception of Galatians: the Law

How far did this short Pauline letter influence the way the Church developed? At the heart of the letter is the question of the nature and authority of the Law of the Jewish scriptures and its continuing role within the life of the Christian Church. How far was it to shape Christian behaviour?

We start with a figure who, though very influential, was regarded by the emerging Great Church as deeply threatening. Marcion (b. *c.*85 in Sinope on the Black Sea) believed that the rulings of the Old Testament law were so harsh that they must come from a different source from the teaching of Jesus and Paul. When Paul and Peter confronted each other at Antioch (Gal. 2:11–16), Marcion argued, they were talking about two different forms of righteousness, derived, whether they knew it or not, from two different divine beings. Peter believed that they both came from the same source and should therefore both be obeyed. Paul, by contrast, saw the law of the Old Testament as a curse and sharply distinguished it from the law of Christ. The old righteousness contrasted with the righteousness of a strange, new, different God of compassion who was revealed in Jesus Christ. So when Paul spoke of two kinds of righteousness (2:16), it was on the basis of a distinction between the God who is good and compassionate *and therefore* just and the Creator of the world, whose justice, because he lacks such compassionate goodness, necessarily turns into harshness, cruelty, and, in consequence of his exclusive love for his chosen people, injustice.

The obvious difficulty with such a reading of Galatians is that in Gal. 3 Paul says that (his) God instituted the Law in order to preserve his people until the coming of Christ. Marcion's answer to this objection is to say that this passage is one of a series of additions which had subsequently been made to the letter (and indeed to the other Christian writings) to bring them into line with the views of the Petrine Church. He consequently produced his own collection of Christian sacred texts, which consisted of edited versions of the Gospel of Luke and ten Pauline letters.

The main body of the Church never accepted Marcion's views. They do nevertheless pose a challenge to all more mainstream interpreters and catch something of the radicalness of Paul's views. What does Paul mean when he refers to the Law as a curse? Could the same God impose such a curse on his people and also show the kind of compassion which is demonstrated on the cross? Marcion's views will continue to challenge interpreters throughout Christian history.

How then did the theologians who laid down the foundations of Christian teaching in the first five centuries and believed that the Law and the New Testament had their source in the same God view the Law and its place in God's dealings with his people? The dominant Christian view, until the time of the Reformation, was that the Law had only a limited role once Christ came. Augustine, writing in North Africa at the end of the 4th century in Latin, says: 'The law was ordained, therefore, for a proud people so that they might be humbled by their transgression . . . so that they might seek grace and not assume that they could be saved by their own merits (which is pride) and so that they might be righteous not by their own power and strength, but by the hand of a mediator who justifies the impious' (*Gal.* 167) This makes it part of God's purposes for leading his people, the Jews, to belief in Christ.

John Chrysostom, writing in Greek at the same time at the other end of the Mediterranean, additionally allows the Law an educative role before the coming of the Spirit in baptism; but its principal function was, temporarily, to restrain: 'that by fear we might chasten our lusts, the Spirit not being manifested'. Once the Spirit comes, which 'not only commands us to abstain from [such lusts] but quenches them and leads us to a higher rule of life', both the Law's educative and disciplinary roles are superseded. 'He who has attained an exalted excellence from an inner impulse, has no occasion for a schoolmaster, nor does anyone, if he is a philosopher, require a grammarian. Why then do you so degrade yourselves, as now to listen to the Law, having previously given yourselves to the Spirit?' (NPNF 13:42) How could the Galatians want to go back to the observation of the Law?

These two enormously influential figures: Augustine for the Christian West, Chrysostom for the East, are writing at a crucial juncture at the end of the 4th century as the old world of paganism gives way to what will become Byzantine and Roman Christianity. At the time it was still by no means finally settled how the profound cultural changes that were occurring would be resolved. Judaism with its ancient customs and scrolls exercised a deep attraction for many and, in consequence, neither Augustine nor Chrysostom had any interest in promoting the importance of the Law. Chrysostom's rejection of it is unequivocal: it has a minor role as moral educator but that is eclipsed by the Spirit, above all by the ascetic disciplines of 4th-/5th-century monasticism. For Augustine, however, the Law does have a continuing role: just as it was intended to drive the Jews to accept Christ, so too the Law by exposing people's sinfulness would drive all people to Christ. Both of them however were agreed that Paul had firmly ruled that the Law was no longer determinative for Christian action.

These ideas would have a long history in Eastern Orthodoxy and in the Christian West. Like Chrysostom, the medieval Western theologian Aquinas would allow that the Old Testament was educative, one source of moral insight along with philosophy (Aristotle) and the New Testament, but certainly not the only or the most important one. The Law for him was also there to restrain sins, to bring people to grace, and to tame concupiscence. The same is to be found in Luther, who as an Augustinian friar draws deeply on Augustine. The Law is a hammer to break the proud. It is also the basis of civil law.

This consensus establishes what came to be referred to as the 'uses of the law'. It has a civil use, to guide the princes in their governance of society; and a theological use, to drive people to Christ. But then a whole new chapter opens after Luther, principally through the writings of John Calvin. Calvin writes as the Reformation takes root in the cities of Europe, in his case in Geneva. The break with Rome has been made. The primacy of scripture over the traditions and teachings of the Church has been asserted and the young Reformed churches turn to the task of creating a new culture and society. Unsurprisingly, in view of the increased authority which they had conferred on scripture, they look to the Old Testament for guidance. In this, they could certainly claim some support from Chrysostom and Aquinas. What is new is the degree of authority with which they invest Old Testament rulings. Appealing to Matthew 5:17: 'Do not think that I have come to abolish the law or the prophets: I have come not to abolish but to fulfil', Calvin argues for a third *and principal* use of the law.

This is addressed to believers that by 'teaching, admonishing, rebuking, and correcting, it [the Law] may fit and prepare us for every good work' (*Inst.* II, 7, 14). The Law, that is, both encourages and instructs believers. 'The laws acts like a whip to the flesh, urging it on as men do a sluggish ass.' And, it is the best instrument for enabling believers, 'in whose hearts the Spirit of God already flourishes and reigns . . . to learn with greater truth and certainty what that will of the Lord is which they aspire to follow, and to confirm them in this knowledge' (*Inst.* II, 7, 12).

The contrast with Chrysostom could not be sharper. For Chrysostom, to subordinate the Spirit to the Law was a form of degradation. For Calvin, faced with radical Reformers who in the Spirit would challenge the rulings of the new church authorities, an appeal to the letter of scripture over the law written in the heart must have seemed like a path to firmer ground. A new era in Reformed theology and practice was dawning, where the rulings of the Old Testament would assume central importance in laying down the legal foundations of the newly emerging political order.

New life in the Spirit: new forms of spirituality

As we have seen, in the last section of the letter, Paul turns to the role of the Spirit in the lives of Christian believers. These two chapters are full of powerful and memorable phrases and have spawned many forms of spirituality. For some they have been an inspiration for cosmological speculation; for others they have fostered forms of inwardness which have left a deep mark on Western culture. They have been drawn on by those who practised various forms of asceticism and monasticism. Equally they have provided encouragement for those who sought to put their faith into practice in everyday life.

5:16–18 reads:

> Live by the Spirit, I say, and do not gratify the desires of the flesh. For what the flesh desires is opposed to the Spirit, and what the Spirit desires is opposed to the flesh; for these are opposed to each other, to prevent you from doing what you want. But if you are led by the Spirit, you are not subject to the law.

Part of the difficulty in interpreting this passage lies partly in the many meanings attaching to the terms flesh and Spirit, partly in what Paul says about them. In what sense are they 'opposed to each other'? And what is the outcome of this opposition? To prevent people doing the good they want? Or the bad? Or, indeed, anything at all?

Dualists, like the Gnostics and Manichaeans who flourished in the early centuries, took flesh and Spirit to refer to two opposed principles in the world which struggled for the control of men and women. The flesh was the manifestation of the principle of evil, contrasted with and wholly distinct from the good God. Buried deep in the heart of men and women, the flesh needs to be rooted out, exposed, and allowed to perish. A 3rd-century Gnostic text, *The Gospel of Philip* enjoins people to 'burrow for the root of evil'. It will be rooted out when it is recognized. Lack of knowledge of evil in non-believers allows it to grow powerful, and is the 'mother of all evils . . . Lack of acquaintance is a slave; acquaintance is freedom' (*Gosp. Phil.* 104). Believers who have knowledge, *gnosis*, enjoy freedom from the evil principle.

For Manichaeans, however, the battle between flesh and Spirit only came to light in the life of the believer. Before then, as most mainstream Christians held, it might appear that the soul is the one who sins, whereas it is the alien principle deep in human beings which forces them to sin. Only when this is understood can the battle begin against the evil principle, through repentance and ascetic practice: abstaining from meat, from procreation, from marriage. Such a pessimistic view of the human predicament casts a long shadow over the life of faith.

John Chrysostom, however, firmly resisted such forms of dualistic speculation: there was only one God and evil was the result of human disobedience. When Paul spoke about the opposition between flesh and Spirit he was referring to two different contrary options (*logismoi*), good and bad, between which the soul has to choose. The opposition is a logical one; choices are set out clearly to the believers so that they can avoid the evil that they are drawn to and instead do good (NPNF 13:41). Christians should counter their inclinations to do evil. Proper self-discipline, found in exemplary form in the life of the desert monks, will deliver a life of goodness.

Augustine, like his Manichaean opponents of whom he had once been a follower, believes that Christians are in the grip of sin. This, however, is not because they are in bondage to an alien principle, but because of 'penal habit', the 'addiction to pleasure that comes about as the penalty . . . of repeated sinning'. The root of sin lies in a human choice, the primal sin of Adam and Eve. Nevertheless those who are under grace do indeed, out of spiritual love, serve the law of God with the mind. The believer was engaged in a constant battle to overcome sinful inclinations: '[o]nly when the body is transformed into an immortal state, will there be no lusts of the flesh' (*Gal.* 211–13).

These readings of Paul provide the basis for a number of very diverse and influential understandings of the human condition. They all grapple with the sense of moral frustration and inner conflict which the commentators, including the more optimistic Chrysostom, experience from their very varied perspectives. They lie at the root of the 'introspective conscience of the West', which at its worst has been experienced as a grave mental affliction, but which equally underlies much of Western thought and literature. Debate rages among scholars as to whether it was Paul or his later followers (Augustine, Luther) who were responsible for this development. Certainly, the reception of texts like Galatians 5:16–18 plays a key role in the development of such profound introspection.

Does Paul offer a way through such problems of moral frustration and inner conflict? If one looks at some of the later interpreters, who have grappled with the darker views of humanity which can be read out of Paul, we can begin to sketch an answer.

Thomas Aquinas, a very close reader of Paul, was alert to the moral tensions highlighted by Paul's interpreters. The flesh and the Spirit are distinct from but not irretrievably opposed to each other. There is a hierarchy in which each has its proper place. The body needs to meet its physical needs, as the mind needs to follow its desire for higher goods. Things go wrong when this hierarchy is disturbed: 'For since the pleasures of the flesh concern goods which are beneath us, whereas the pleasures of the spirit concern goods which are above us . . . when the soul is occupied with the lower things of the flesh, it is withdrawn from the higher things of the spirit' (*Gal.* 168–9). Getting the soul to fix its gaze on things above requires, as Chrysostom had said, spiritual discipline, fasting, vigils. Such serious human effort, assisted by the Spirit, forms habits of virtue in the soul countering the sinful habits which so concerned Augustine.

Martin Luther was an Augustinian canon (monk). Augustine's emphasis on the 'penal habit' of sin, coupled with medieval portrayals of the Last Judgement and the fate of the damned, led to unbearable anxiety in Luther. He eventually found release in his understanding of the term the 'righteousness of God'. When Paul talked about God's righteousness, he didn't mean the righteousness which people achieved through their own efforts, according to which God would judge them; he meant the righteousness which God conferred on believers as a gift. This was the gift of a new life, freed from fear, based on trust in God's mercy and compassion, which made it possible for people from all areas of life, not just monks, to 'walk by the Spirit'. They might never fulfil all that the Law required; nevertheless they should 'endeavour [them]selves diligently to walk in the Spirit' and in this way fulfil Christ's command to love each other.

This is surprisingly similar to what Aquinas had said. If anything, the emphasis on human effort, '*endeavour yourselves diligently to walk* in the Spirit' is greater than in Aquinas. However this no longer refers principally to the battle against carnal desire experienced by 'hermits and monks' but to the whole sphere of human activity in the world.

> So the prince fulfilleth not the concupiscence of the flesh, when he diligently doth his duty and governeth his subjects well. . . . Here the flesh and the devil resist, and tempt him, provoking him to make unrighteous war, to obey his own covetousness, &c; and except he follow the leading of the Spirit and obey the good and holy admonitions of the Word of God concerning his office, then he fulfilleth the lusts of the flesh, &c. So let every man in his calling

walk in the Spirit, and he shall not fulfil either his carnal lust or any other of the works of the flesh. (*LW* 27:69–70)

The new life in Christ is for every man and woman 'in their calling'. Christian living no longer finds its exemplary form in a life cloistered from the world but in the lives of the faithful prince, merchant, servant, wife, husband, child in the world. This represents a radical attempt to place religion at the heart of ordinary life. The transformation of the individual's personal relationship with God frees him or her to see the world of commerce and politics and social and family life as the proper field for the exercise of Christian love.

Not all Luther's followers embraced his call to pursue their vocations in civil society. Many were drawn back into the introspective, anxious world of the young Augustinian monk and failed to find escape from the terrors which tormented him. The films of Ingmar Bergman, and Gabriel Axel's *Babette's Feast*, based on an Isak Dinesen short story, give telling portrayals of such forms of Lutheranism. Against this needs to be set the immense liberation that Luther's writing brought to the late medieval world, to the extraordinary energy released into the lives of late medieval cities, and the growth of enterprise which occurred as secular vocations gained recognition as fully Christian forms of life. Spirituality was redefined and the lives of lay people given their full value within the world of faith.

Luther's commentary on Galatians itself, published in English in 1575, certainly brought such release. John Bunyan, the great Puritan writer of *Pilgrim's Progress* (1678), wrote: 'I do prefer this book of Martin Luther upon the Galatians, excepting the Bible, before all books that I have ever seen, as most fit for a wounded conscience.' On Whitsunday 1738, Charles Wesley was converted by reading the preface to Luther's Galatians commentary: 'From this time forward I endeavoured to ground as many of our friends who came into this fundamental truth, salvation by faith alone, not an idle, dead faith but a faith which works by love, and is necessarily productive of all good works and all holiness.' For Bunyan and Charles Wesley, and for many of their readers and disciples, here was indeed a new creative world.

Much more could be said about the ways in which Galatians has helped to shape very different societies. In Chapter 9 we shall look at the ways in which Christian believers have grappled with the conflicts that can occur between their deepest convictions and the laws of the state, as we will look at the way that Gal. 3:28 has influenced recent discussions of identity politics. We should not really be surprised that such a powerful and suggestive text, written out of a moment of intense struggle for the heart of a fledgling religious movement, has had such widely diverse readings. For many, its appeal has lain in its ability to spark renewal and transformation. Figures like Chrysostom and Augustine and Luther ushered in new worlds with profound consequences for later generations. Part of the text's power lies in the clean break which it makes with the old world out of which the new is emerging. Believers in Christ must turn their back on the Law. Not to do so is to remain caught in the old and to deny the new experience which they have already tasted in the Spirit. Here the text has broad normative force.

This negative ruling then enables believers to enjoy the freedom to explore the new worlds which are dawning. And it allows full rein to Paul's imagery and rhetoric, his ability to forge new concepts and awaken hope and desire for the new, for liberation and the simple virtues of 'love, joy, peace, patience, kindness, generosity, faithfulness, gentleness and self-control' (Gal. 5:22–3). All this has a formative power which is rare among literary documents of any kind. The forms of life and society which have emerged may not always have developed as their original movers may have wished but they have had extraordinary vigour and creativity. Paul's letter remains for many a source of renewal and hope.

Chapter 7
The Bible and its critics

At the beginning of the modern period, the Bible begins to move out of the close control of the Church. Its influence grows. Its effects are felt more at all levels of society, by those inside and outside the—now very many—different churches. And the Bible comes under closer scrutiny and criticism.

Criticism at root refers to the exercise of one's judgement. In effect, all interpreters of the Bible use their judgement to discriminate between possible meanings and senses of the text. They may well also want to give more weight to certain passages than others, to find meaningful interpretations for passages which seem to be of little obvious interest or whose apparent sense seems contradictory to expectation. This kind of intelligent, discriminating reading has been a perennial feature of scriptural interpretation and is at the basis of present standard historical disciplines of text criticism, source criticism, and various forms of literary criticism, with which (almost) all biblical scholars work. However, the term 'biblical criticism' can also have a much more antagonistic sense, when it is directed against dominant, ecclesiastical understandings of the Bible. Many of the developments which I will sketch out belong to this category. Much of what is now standard critical practice was in fact pioneered by those who used it to attack mainstream church readings.

Such developments need to be set in their historical context. By the end of the Middle Ages, Christian interpretation of the Bible was more or less integrated with the official ideology of the Church. The Bible contained stories about the creation of the world, the history of the patriarchs, the election of Israel and the giving of the Law, the subsequent history of Israel in the Land, together with stories about Jesus and the early Christian missionary efforts and controversies. All this had been read in such a way as to give an integrated—and comprehensive—world history from the creation until the final judgement. The Bible, the Church taught, told the story of God's response to Adam's sin: through the election of Israel and the giving of the Law, culminating in the sending of his son, the redemption of humanity through his crucifixion and resurrection, and the establishment of the Church. In such a reading of the Bible, elements which play a central role in the Old Testament were played down: the giving of the Land, the Temple, the role of the Law and Israel in the salvation of the nations. Equally, motifs which are relatively minor were stressed, notably the notion of the Fall and of the universal corruption of the human race. The Old Testament was read as a precursor for the New, its main figures and their lives anticipating what was now fully realized in Jesus (as we saw with the comparison which the Fathers made between Isaac and Christ).

Thanks to the construction of this all-embracing narrative, the Bible became the source and measure of all knowledge: of cosmology, of history, of law, and of theology. In working such a story out, the theologians were, it is true, assisted by other disciplines. The Church Fathers of the first centuries drew freely on the Platonist philosophers; the medieval Schoolmen, not without controversy, drew on Aristotle. But, officially at least, the Bible remained the final arbiter of truth. There was, seemingly, a remarkable fit between the Bible and the world in which medieval Christians lived. The Renaissance and the Reformation would, however, launch a two-pronged attack on this official consensus in the European West.

The Church under attack: challenges from within

The Christian story just outlined was not the only Christian version. There were deviant views within the Church, which had itself split into East and West at the end of the previous millennium. The criticisms of the Christian story in the late medieval period had a broad base. Much criticism came from within and was directed against the narrative's biblical basis. Luther's Reformation was the work of a professor of biblical studies. He used his formidable skills in reading ancient biblical texts, not only to make the Bible widely available in the vernacular, but also to challenge the accepted biblical world-view at a particularly sensitive point.

In one sense this was only a matter of minor changes to certain aspects of the overall picture, relating particularly to the role of the Church in the salvation of individual souls. Late medieval doctrine taught that because God was a just judge, men and women, though redeemed by Christ's work, would still have to pay the penalty for their sins on earth; they could avoid or mitigate their justly deserved punishment, however, even after death, if they made use of the various penitential offices of the Church. 2 Maccabees 12:43–5 offered scriptural support for prayers for the dead. The widespread acceptance of such doctrines bestowed enormous authority on the ecclesiastical hierarchy.

Luther (see Figure 3) challenged this perception of God's justice and forgiveness by scrutinizing its roots in scripture, notably in the Pauline epistles. The key text for him was in the Epistle to the Romans: 'For in it the righteousness of God is revealed through faith for faith; as it is written, "He who through faith is righteous shall live."' (Romans 1:17, quoting Habakkuk 2:4.) But what precisely did St Paul mean, asked Luther, when he talked about the righteousness of God which was revealed by the Gospel? Did he refer, as the Scholastics taught, to the righteous nature of God's

3. Portrait of Martin Luther, the Professor of Biblical Studies whose interpretation of Paul was the catalyst for the Protestant Reformation.

handing out of justice, by which he condemns sinners and rewards the righteous? Or did he refer to the gift of righteousness which God conferred on unrighteous men and women? Either understanding could be supported by the Greek expression; what was decisive was the context in Romans, where Paul quotes a phrase from Habakkuk. It refers, Luther claims, to the gift of righteousness to those who believe, and who will in consequence have life.

This is a defining moment in the Reformation, and indeed in European history. For Luther the Bible now speaks about the liberation of men and women from the threat of God's law and punishment. It speaks about the grace and forgiveness of God given to all who hear the gospel, and not just to those who submit to the penitential discipline of the Church. In this way the Reformation sought to emancipate men and women from their bondage to the medieval Church; they were now free to follow their vocations in the 'worldly kingdom'.

Thus this provocative new reading of the Pauline epistles provided the basis for a major transformation of the power structures and general ethos and attitudes of medieval Europe. What is interesting for our purposes here is how it was achieved. Luther argued against the dominant scholastic interpretation by appealing to the 'grammatical sense' of scripture. That is to say, he used the standard methods of humanist philology and textual study to resolve what was an ambiguity within the Pauline text. In this way, reasoned, critical study of Paul was used to unseat the dominant, official understanding of the text.

Luther's critique of the dominant understanding of the Bible was applied from within the Church. His pre-eminence within Protestantism would mean that such use of critical reason would become an essential (if not always exercised) characteristic of Protestant theology. In time, the range of critical methodologies would be expanded: historical, sociological, and literary criticisms would follow. Such exercise of critical reason would, of course, create yet more diversity of interpretation and the risk of still greater disunity. However powerful the orthodoxies which from time to time gripped Protestantism, the critical spirit would always be there, ready to subvert and loosen their hold.

The Church under attack: challenges from without

Not all challenges to the received interpretation of the Bible came from within the Church. The explosion of human knowledge and discovery which marked the end of the Middle Ages provided challenges of its own to a world-view which had been proclaimed to be all-encompassing and authoritative. In the first place, the discovery of new lands, broadcast in popular travellers' tales, showed up the geographical limitations of the biblical world-view. There were whole continents which had not even been dreamt of in the account of the world which had been spun out of the biblical narratives. Even if, by vigorous missionary activity, such lands could now be incorporated within Christendom, there remained a lasting question about the place which the new converts' forebears had had within God's universal plan of salvation.

Furthermore, the growth of historical sciences made it clear that the Bible's view of history was far from comprehensive. Historical research undermined the chronology of the Bible; it uncovered evidence of the existence of earlier civilizations not known to the biblical writers. And the historical schema found in the Bible simply failed to encompass subsequent history. Daniel 7 speaks of four kingdoms and this, at the time of the Reformation, was widely adopted as a framework for world history. The four kingdoms were identified as those of the Chaldaeans, the Persians, Alexander the Great, and the Romans. The question was what had become of the Roman Empire? The German emperor claimed the title of Holy Roman Emperor, but where did that leave the French king—as his permanent vassal? It is not difficult to see the attractions to those who sought political security of the idea of a final (and therefore humanly unassailable) empire before the advent of Christ. But, like all attempts to stop the historical clock, it would hardly stand the test of time. Empires would come and go and the schema outlined in Daniel would simply not be complex or flexible enough to contain them.

If the view of history constructed out of the Bible was vulnerable to attack, then so too was its cosmology. Copernicus taught that the planets, including the earth, revolved around the sun. In the strange and bloodthirsty story in Joshua 10, Joshua, with the armies of the five kings of the Amorites at his mercy, prays to God, 'Sun, stand thou still upon Gibeon; and thou, Moon, in the valley of Ajalon' (10:12). The prayer is answered: the sun and moon stand still for about a day, while Joshua's armies slaughter their opponents. The conflict between the cosmology in this story and Copernicus' understanding of planetary movements is clear. Even Luther and his disciple Melanchthon use the biblical story to dismiss the views of Copernicus. At this time, to all except a few mathematicians, Copernicus' theory of the revolution of the celestial bodies would have seemed just one among many speculations. Melanchthon, citing a number of biblical passages, including Joshua 10:12–13, categorically rejects Copernicus: 'Strengthened by these divine testimonies, we hold fast to the truth and do not allow ourselves to be led astray from it by the blind works of those who think it the glory of the intellect to confuse the free arts'. The theologian Andreas Osiander, who prepared an edition of Copernicus' work published in Nuremberg in 1543, recognized the seriousness of Copernicus' challenge and attempted to soften its offensiveness by arguing that Copernicus' views were mere hypotheses, useful for predicting the positions of the planets, but not intended to be factual statements about the workings of the universe. Such calculations were of great practical value; knowledge of the true causes of the movements of heavenly bodies is beyond the reach of our minds.

Later debates between Darwinists and Creationists in the 19th century continued the same theme: Darwin's view of the origin of humankind in a line of mammals running through the apes clearly provided a very different account of human origins from that in Genesis. Notwithstanding the internal contradictions of the two accounts in Genesis 1 and 2, many Christians held that the Genesis account of direct divine intervention to create human beings should be treated as authoritative. Others came to see the Genesis stories as creation myths, not unrelated to other myths of this kind which circulated in the world of the Ancient Near East. This of course raised important questions about the relation of such myths to the scientific world-view.

The Enlightenment and the rise of historical criticism

The internal church divisions of the Reformation period eventually led to religious wars which ravaged Europe from 1618 to 1648. This in turn led to a fierce reaction against all forms of religion and a search for emancipation from its authority, which is broadly referred to as the Enlightenment. The same period saw the rise of the empirical sciences and of rationalist and empiricist philosophies which sought to base human knowledge and the conduct of human affairs on the unaided efforts of human reason. Such philosophies were powerful tools in the hands of those who sought political liberation in the absolutist states of Europe, whose authority rested on alliances with different churches. Human knowledge, said the French philosopher Descartes, himself a devout Catholic, should be based not on inherited beliefs and authority, but on 'clear and distinct ideas', which could be discerned only by subjecting all our beliefs to radical scrutiny.

One quite diverse group of critics in England was known as the Deists. They sought to exclude religion from the management of human affairs. God, they said, was a distant figure who had created the world and then left it to its own devices, a watchmaker who had wound up the watch and then left it to run according to its own laws. They attacked the Bible, partly because it contained stories of divine interference with the operation of the physical ('natural') laws of the universe; and partly because it sought to impose a supposedly divinely instituted system of laws which were contrary to natural morality. In consequence, they ridiculed the miracle stories of the Bible, and attacked the morality of its main protagonists. They also attacked the doctrines by which orthodox Christians defined the authority of the Bible as the supreme vehicle of divine revelation and as such incapable of error. They pointed to the existence of inconsistencies and contradictions within the Bible itself. A lively literature grew up around the resurrection narratives. In its more colourful forms, the apostles were imagined in a trial setting and subjected to cross-examination to see if their case could be demolished. The finest example of this genre is Thomas Sherlock's 1729 'Trial of the Witnesses'.

Such literature was disseminated relatively freely in Britain in the 18th century and found its way to France and Germany, where, however, draconian censorship curbed its distribution. This provides the setting for one of the more dramatic events in the history of biblical criticism, the so-called 'battle of the Fragments'. The main protagonists on the rationalist side in this dispute were a Hamburg scholar-schoolmaster, Hermann Samuel Reimarus, and Gotthold Ephraim Lessing, a playwright, literary critic, and philosopher-theologian. The two met when Lessing was in charge of the theatre in Hamburg. From there he moved to the Duke of Brunswick's library at Wolfenbüttel, using his position to publish anonymously parts, 'Fragments', of a work by Reimarus. These appeared in instalments: starting with material closely related to the work of the Deists and then in 1778 a section entitled 'Of the Purpose of Jesus and his disciples'.

In the first two paragraphs Jesus is portrayed as the preacher of a purified natural religion. Like the Pharisees, says Reimarus, Jesus taught the doctrine of immortality. Unlike them he taught a righteousness purged of outward observance and free of hypocrisy. But then quite suddenly Reimarus introduces a question of a completely different kind: 'Just as then there can be no doubt that Jesus pointed men in his teaching to the true great purpose of religion, namely eternal blessedness, so then it remains only to ask what purpose Jesus had for himself in his teaching and actions.'

The question—what purpose did Jesus have for himself?—is certainly unusual. As the sequel makes clear, what Reimarus is asking about is Jesus's engagement with the pressing concerns of his day: about Jewish aspirations for independence from Roman rule, about political power and its control and distribution. This was revolutionary. Earlier views of Jesus had portrayed him as a heavenly figure who had come to reveal heavenly mysteries and to institute a new religion. Such a revealed religion, which was beyond the reach of human reason, sat easily with contemporary authoritarian politics. The questions Reimarus posed about Jesus's involvement in the hopes, fears, and aspirations of people in the 1st century put Jesus back into the sphere of human history and politics. There are echoes here of Luther's 'secularization' of Christian belief, taking Christian belief and practice outside the private realm of the cloister and planting it in the sphere of everyday life. Such questions endangered the neat separation of the spheres of influence of Church and state in Lutheranism, where the Church was responsible for men and women's supernatural goals and for the rest gave unquestioned support to the secular rulers. Could it be, as Reimarus suggested, that when Jesus announced the coming kingdom of God, he was referring to the political overthrow of the ruling power, the Romans? In view of such disturbing political overtones in the published Fragments, the Imperial Censor prohibited Lessing from making any further contribution to what had become a major public debate.

The questions Reimarus raised were, in the first place, historical questions, requiring all the tools available to the historian to answer them. Reimarus, in a remarkable way, spelled out some of the main tasks which such an enquiry into the life and thought of Jesus would involve. One would need to scrutinize the main sources for his life, the first three Gospels, to see to what extent they had been subject to later revision and distortion. One would have to pay close attention to the contemporary sense of words and phrases. Jesus told his contemporaries to expect the coming of the 'kingdom of God'. But what did such a claim mean to Jesus's hearers?

The publication of Reimarus' work inaugurated a remarkably fruitful period of study, which Albert Schweitzer documented at the beginning of the 20th century in his classic work, *The Quest for the Historical Jesus*. What becomes clear in the course of this enquiry is the central importance of trying to place Jesus firmly in the context of 1st-century religious beliefs and movements. The effort required for such a historical investigation was, and still is, enormous. One has only to think of the work that has been undertaken since 1948 in deciphering, translating, and editing the Dead Sea Scrolls to realize how much work is involved in preparing scholarly editions of the large number of relevant texts, even before the task of interpreting them and placing Jesus in relation to them can begin. The complexity of the task is further increased by the geographical spread of the sources and influences involved. On the one hand, the texts of the Old Testament have their roots in the wider world of the Ancient Near East; on the other, Christianity rapidly expanded into the Graeco-Roman world of the Mediterranean outside Roman Palestine. To understand fully Jesus's place in the history of the development of religious belief and practice in the ancient world one needs a truly formidable knowledge. Such an undertaking can only be a communal one.

Yet even once scholars have begun to develop a reasonably reliable picture of the religious beliefs and practices of Jesus's day, how is one to use that knowledge to give a clearer account of Jesus's 'purpose'? Was Jesus an 'apocalyptic' figure, who looked for a sudden divine intervention in the course of history, where the old age would be swept away and a new age, 'the kingdom of God', ushered in? Or was he, rather, a purveyor of peasant wisdom, assisting his followers to make sense of a troubled and troubling world? Some have suggested that when he spoke of the establishment of God's rule, he was not so much referring to the establishing of some kind of new socio-political order but rather expressing views closer to the rabbinic notion of the acceptance by the individual of God's will. Some have (rather unpersuasively) even wanted to place Jesus closer to 1st-century liberationist groups who sought to establish God's rule and Israel's independence by military means. Answers to these questions remain elusive.

What such discussions do however bring home is the extent to which the biblical texts and the figures who feature in them belong to a particular age and culture often very different, and indeed alien, to our own. Albert Schweitzer famously described this sense of the strangeness of the Jesus uncovered by the historical quest:

> The study of the Life of Jesus has had a curious history. It set out in quest of the historical Jesus, believing that when it had found Him it could bring Him straight into our time as a Teacher and Saviour. It loosed the bands by which He had been riveted for centuries to the stony rocks of ecclesiastical doctrine, and rejoiced to see life and movement coming into the figure once more, and the historical Jesus advancing, as it seemed, to meet it. But He does not stay; He passes by our time and returns to His own.
>
> (*The Quest for the Historical Jesus*, p. 397)

For Schweitzer, this is not all loss. We may not be able to turn Jesus into a figure easily recognizable to us. Just as he does not fit easily into traditional doctrinal categorizations, so he eludes our attempts to modernize him, to co-opt him for our own aims. 'We can find no designation which expresses what he is for us.' But he remains a commanding figure, who can make claims on us and call us to new tasks:

> He comes to us as One unknown, without a name, as of old, by the lake-side, He came to those who knew Him not. He speaks to us the same word: 'Follow thou me!' and sets us to the tasks which He has to fulfil for our time. He commands. And to those who obey Him, whether they be wise or simple, He will reveal Himself in the toils, the conflicts and the sufferings which they shall pass through in His fellowship, and, as an ineffable mystery, they shall learn in their own experience Who He is.
>
> (*The Quest for the Historical Jesus*, p. 410)

Criticism and creative readings

We have looked at critics both within and outside the Church as they sought to prise the Bible away from received church interpretations. Such interpretations sought to bring the text and the experience of believers into a creative and harmonious relation. The main criticisms came from those whose experience could no longer be accommodated within the Church's biblical story. History, geography, and theories of evolution all burst the bounds of such interpretation. But if the Bible is prised away from its received interpretations, this does not mean that it ceases to be a source of social and cultural creativity. On the contrary, such fierce criticism of received interpretations can prepare the way for new and creative readings of the Bible. In their different ways, both Luther and those who engaged in the quest for the historical Jesus were seeking to make the Bible their own. Luther dramatically succeeded and thereby inaugurated a new family of Protestant readings. The work of the historical critics in attempting to reconstruct the life and teaching of Jesus—surely one of the most sustained intellectual undertakings in the world of the arts—has in turn generated a great diversity of readings of the Gospels. This process of historical quest and reconstruction ends with a much greater sense of the culturally conditioned nature of both the text and any subsequent interpretation. This has a twofold effect. On the one hand it issues a challenge to all attempts to equate the meaning of the Bible with any given interpretation. On the other, an awareness that the biblical texts themselves are the result of a creative dialogue between ancient traditions and different communities through the ages may be a spur to further attempts to read the Bible creatively and imaginatively in contemporary contexts.

Chapter 8
The Bible in the post-colonial world

The areas of greatest growth for Christianity today are in Africa, Asia, and South America, in countries emerging from a prolonged period of colonial domination, but often still dominated by economically more powerful nations and transnational institutions. Here the Bible is playing a remarkable role in the growth of new churches and new forms of church life. It has inspired struggles for liberation from oppressive regimes and has provided rich material for those seeking to develop forms of Christianity closer to their own traditional cultures. As the Bible has been translated into the vernacular, so new forms of belief and practice have grown up alongside the mainstream mission churches.

In all this, the uses to which the Bible is being put are by no means uncontested. The Bible was used by colonizers and missionaries in ways which were often far from liberating or respectful of local culture. This chapter will attempt to illustrate some of these very different readings and to identify the different socio-cultural phenomena which have contributed to their development.

The Bible in Latin America

The colonization of Latin America is one of the darkest episodes in European history. In the first hundred years after Columbus' arrival, millions of people died through war, disease, and ill-treatment. In some areas the population was reduced by 80 per cent. The Spaniards and Portuguese who colonized Central and South America were 'given' the land by the Pope and encouraged to convert its population. Columbus (see Figure 4), who arrived in the Americas in 1492, believed that his mission was part of the dawning of a new age, when the whole world would be united in Christ under the Pope to enjoy the final millennium before the Last Judgement. He was fond of quoting Isaiah 65:17: 'For I am about to create new heavens and a new earth'; and its echo in Revelation 21:1. The new age would embrace the whole earth; Mount Zion would be regained for Christianity and all would acknowledge the one true faith.

A papal decree commanded the monarchs of Spain and Portugal to wage a holy war to support this missionary endeavour. Here the narratives of the conquest of Canaan in Joshua and Judges provided support not only for conquest, but also for the merciless killing of those who refused to submit. As one contemporary commentator on the widespread deaths, Fray Toribio, put it,

> Whether or not the great sins and idolatries that took place in this land cause it [the dying], I do not know; nevertheless I see that those seven idolatrous generations that possessed the promised land were destroyed by Joshua and then the children of Israel populated it.

It is then not surprising that there have been those who have seen the Bible wholly as an instrument of oppression. When the Pope visited Peru, he received an open letter from various indigenous groups, inviting him to take back the Bible to Europe.

> John Paul II, we Andean and American Indians, have decided to take advantage of your visit to return to you your Bible, since in five centuries it has not given us love, peace, or justice.
>
> Please take back your Bible and give it back to our oppressors, because they need its moral teachings more than we do.

4. First Landing of Christopher Columbus. By Frederick Kemmelmeyer.

Nevertheless, Latin America also saw a powerful movement arise to rescue the Bible from its colonial misuse. Even at the time of the conquistadores there were voices which appealed to the Bible against the appalling treatment of the Indians. Of course, the Bible was not needed to show that the treatment of the Indians was unjust and cruel beyond compare, but its authority could be invoked to oppose the oppressive treatment of the indigenous peoples. Bartolomé de Las Casas, the first priest ordained in the New World, a chaplain to the Spanish armies which conquered Cuba (1513), and a one-time slave-owner, became a resolute opponent of the Spanish conquest. He appealed to Sirach 34:21–6: 'The bread of the needy is the life of the poor; whoever deprives them of it, is a man of blood. To take away a neighbour's living is to murder him; to deprive an employee of his wages is to shed blood.' In his sermon at Pentecost in 1514, he asserted that an offering made to God without the practice of justice was stained with the blood of the poor: 'Like one who kills a son before his father's eyes is the man who offers a sacrifice from the property of the poor.' He was eventually ordered to withdraw to a monastery, attacked by his enemies as a heretic, and had his confessional withdrawn by the Emperor Charles V. Subsequently, Philip II of Spain approved measures to confiscate his works.

This same emphasis on viewing reality from the perspective of the poor is found in the work of contemporary Latin American liberation theologians. It finds expression in their claims that God is on the side of the poor and that the Church must therefore espouse a 'preferential option for the poor'; and in the belief that the spiritual resources of the poor will provide a vital source of renewal for the Church.

In *A Theology of Liberation* (1971), the Peruvian Indian priest Gustavo Gutiérrez reviews nearly 500 years of colonization and Western dominance. The vast mass of the population live in great poverty; the indigenous population are largely confined to the rural areas or the margins of the big cities. But for Gutiérrez the

Bible speaks of liberation—'For freedom Christ has set us free' (Galatians 5:1)—and such freedom must embrace political and economic freedom. In his preaching Paul reminds us of 'the passage from the old man to the new, from sin to grace, from slavery to freedom'. But when he talks about freedom, he is referring to 'liberation from sin insofar as it represents a selfish turning in upon oneself... [B]ehind an unjust structure there is a personal or collective will responsible—a willingness to reject God and neighbour. It suggests, likewise, that a social transformation, no matter how radical it may be, does not automatically achieve the suppression of all evils' (*A Theology of Liberation*, p. 35).

Liberation theology is an attempt to enlarge theology to take into account the social and political dimensions of human existence and so to reflect on the nature of the transformation required to bring about a just and peaceful world. Such transformation must by definition be social, a transformation of the structures and forms of society. But it cannot stop there: if it is to bring lasting peace and justice it requires an individual and collective change of heart.

This shift of theology from the sphere of private, individual salvation to the public and the social is the characteristic mark of liberation theology. It is grounded in a consideration of the nature of God as revealed in the narratives of the Bible, notably in the narratives of the Exodus, the Passion, and the resurrection. Exodus speaks of God's response to the cries of his people in Egypt, suffering under slavery; the narrative of the death and resurrection of Jesus speaks of a hope for the transformation of the whole of human existence.

The choice of the Exodus narrative, of Israel's liberation from slavery in Egypt and subsequent entry into a 'land flowing with milk and honey', is an obvious one: it speaks of a God who 'takes the part of the oppressed... God's impartiality makes God love the orphan and the widow with preference. Curiously, but nevertheless logically, not making exception of persons means making a preferential option in a situation of oppression' (Pixley, *On Exodus*, p. 232, with reference to Deuteronomy 10:16–18).

If the choice of Exodus is an obvious one, it is also problematic, not least in the post-colonial situation of Latin America. For these narratives are closely linked with the narratives of the conquest of Canaan, which provided the ideological material for the colonial exploitation of Latin America, and indeed of other parts of the world. Some principle of selection is required if the narrative of liberation is not to end up as a narrative of conquest and genocide.

Pixley and Gutiérrez take different routes. Pixley, following the United States theologian Norman Gottwald, offers a reconstructed history of Israel. This supplements and clarifies, rather than strictly contradicting, what is indicated in the Bible. In Gottwald's view, Israel developed out of a conglomerate of tribes in the 'least populated' mountain areas of Palestine, who had migrated internally, fleeing the oppressive and warring kingdoms in the coastal plains. These were subsequently joined by the Hebrews who had escaped from Egyptian domination and these different groups eventually linked together in their belief in Yahweh, the God of the Hebrews. The narratives of the conquest and the destruction of the Canaanites are dismissed as later constructions. At the theological core of the narrative is the belief in the liberator, Yahweh. 'The fact that they succeeded in escaping enforced serfdom despite the powerful Egyptian army showed that God, who took the side of the poor in Egypt, was the true God' (Pixley, *On Exodus*, p. 236).

Gutiérrez stays closer to the biblical text, but does so selectively. In his biblical meditation, *The God of Life*, there is no reference at all to the book of Joshua. What he does is to juxtapose the Exodus narrative with the preaching of Jesus and in particular his reading of Isaiah at his initial sermon in Luke's Gospel (4:18):

> The Spirit of the Lord is upon me,
> because he has anointed me to bring good news to the poor.
> He has sent me to proclaim release to the captives and
> recovery of sight to the blind, to let the oppressed go free.

Read through this lens, the narratives of the conquest of the land simply disappear; or, to put it another way, Jesus's sermon, with its weighting of the Old Testament traditions, itself provides a (canonical) principle of selection for the reading of the whole Bible. This contrasts with Gottwald's attempt to use historical reconstruction to correct/sanitize the biblical narratives.

The Bible in Africa

Colonialism in Africa extends into the very recent past. Most countries gained their independence only after the Second World War. In Africa too the Bible could be used both as an instrument of oppression and of liberation. In South Africa, the stories of the Exodus and the entry to the Promised Land played a significant part in the emerging ideology of Afrikanerdom. As the British took over the running of the Cape from the early Dutch colonizers and enforced their own legislation and taxation, Afrikaners began to leave and to set up new republics in Natal, the Orange Free State, and the Transvaal. It was easy for them to see such movements in terms taken from the Old Testament: they were fleeing from the British yoke, heading to the Promised Land which God had given to them. The fact that one of their grievances was that the British refused to let them keep slaves did not stop them drawing such parallels. Nor is slavery as an institution condemned in the Old Testament. Relatively enlightened laws in the Pentateuch seek to regulate but not to abolish it.

Later Afrikaner ideology saw the Great Trek as a pilgrimage from bondage of a people 'peculiar to God', pursued by the British army, into the land of promise, beset on all sides by unbelieving black 'Canaanites'. Thus a racist element is introduced into the appropriation of the texts. The identification of the black population with the Canaanites, in contrast to the white Afrikaners as God's peculiar people, sets a permanent barrier between the two peoples.

Such readings of the Bible did not go unchallenged. While much of the opposition to apartheid was based on secular ideologies, church leaders like Desmond Tutu (see Figure 5) could address the Afrikaner leaders on a particularly sensitive point: their use of the biblical traditions.

Tutu contests apartheid land policy, specifically the policy of clearing blacks from their traditional lands and relocating them in the so-called homelands. While Afrikaners saw the black population as 'Canaanites' cast out of their land because of their

5. Desmond Tutu.

lawlessness, Tutu portrayed the black inhabitants of Duncan Village, who were under threat of forced removal, in terms of the narrative of Naboth's vineyard. In the story in 1 Kings 21, Ahab, the king of Samaria, offers to buy or to exchange the vineyard of one of his subjects, Naboth. Naboth refuses, because it is 'the inheritance of his fathers'. Jezebel, Ahab's foreign wife, intervenes and arranges to have Naboth falsely accused and stoned. When Ahab goes to take possession of the vineyard he is met by Elijah the prophet, who proclaims God's judgement on him in suitably colourful terms: 'In the place where dogs licked up the blood of Naboth, dogs will also lick up your blood' (21:19).

It is easy for Tutu to draw the parallels between Naboth and the villagers, and between Ahab and Jezebel and the South African regime. The latter are the powerful who think they can treat the villagers as 'unimportant people... You are nobodies in this country, this land of your birth.' But 'God cares about injustice, about oppression, about exploitation.' What the regime portrays as a matter of racial policy, of separate development, Tutu presents uncompromisingly as a matter of injustice, of disregard for the dignity of the blacks. 'There is enough land for everybody in South Africa. It is just that some people are greedy and at the moment they are also powerful, and so they can satisfy their greed at the expense of others who they think to be unimportant and without power. But these are they whom God supports. South Africa, please remember the story of Naboth's vineyard' (Tutu, *Hope and Suffering*, p. 42). The unspoken details of the Naboth story give Tutu's references to it an edge, almost an element of threat. It is not difficult to see why white South Africans reacted so powerfully against Tutu.

Tutu had already spoken powerfully on the subject of land-rights in his open letter to John Vorster, the then Prime Minister, whom he addresses

> as one human person to another human person, gloriously created in the image of the self-same Son of God [Romans 8:29] who for all

> our sakes died on the cross and rose triumphant from the dead...sanctified by the self-same Spirit who works inwardly in all of us to change our hearts of stone into hearts of flesh [Ezekiel 36:26; 2 Corinthians 3:3]...as one Christian to another, for through our common baptism we have been made members of and are united in the Body of our dear Lord and Saviour, Jesus Christ [1 Corinthians 12:13]. This Jesus Christ, whatever we may have done, has broken down all that separates us irrelevantly—such as race, sex, culture, status, etc. [Ephesians 2:14; Galatians 3:28]. In this Jesus Christ we are for ever bound together as one redeemed humanity, Black and White together. (*Hope and Suffering*, p. 29)

The language is shot through with biblical echoes and allusions, creating a canonical framework within which to read the Bible. Rather than picking one leading theme, be it Exodus or possession of the Land, Tutu draws widely on themes from the Old and the New Testaments to provide a pattern of shared, basic beliefs. The racism of the Afrikaner readings of the conquest narratives is replaced with a Christian universalism, where social divisions are set aside in favour of a common humanity 'in Christ'.

Post-independence African readings

What happens when the colonial yoke is thrown off? How can the African churches, established and long run by Western missionaries, develop a theology and spirituality which is genuinely African in its expression and social embodiment? What contribution can the Bible make to this undertaking? The question of inculturation, of the rooting of Christianity in African culture, has engaged both the mainstream churches and those which have broken away, the African Independent Churches (AICs).

Musa Dube from Botswana recounts how AIC women in her country read the story of Jesus's encounter with a Canaanite woman, Matthew 15:21–8. The woman comes to Jesus asking him to heal her daughter, who is possessed. Jesus initially turns her away, claiming that he is 'sent only to the lost sheep of the house of Israel', and saying: 'It is not fair to take the children's food and throw it to the dogs.' However, the woman's reply—'Yes, Lord, yet even the dogs eat the crumbs which fall from their master's table'—is met with Jesus's praise of her faith and agreement to her request.

The African women's readings of this story were striking in a number of ways. They are all based in a strong belief in Moya, Spirit. The Spirit empowers people 'to prophesy, heal the sick, assist those searching for jobs, restore family relations, ensure good harvest, good rains, and good reproduction of livestock, and to dispel the ever-intruding forces of evil from people's lives' (Dube, 'Readings of *Semoya*', p. 112). So it is the Spirit, they said, which leads Jesus to the encounter with the woman; it is the work of the Spirit that Jesus should heal, teach, and preach. Moreover, the Spirit is for them inclusive. The AICs grew out of a rejection of 'the discriminative leadership of missionary churches... Moya revealed to them the beauty of the gospel, its justice, and its inclusiveness over against the discriminative tendencies of the colonial church' ('Readings of *Semoya*', p. 124). Strikingly, one of the women explained the relation of Canaanites and Israelites as follows: '"Israelites were taken from Egypt, where they were enslaved... and sent to Canaan, a land flowing with milk and honey. This Canaanite woman with great faith illustrates for us what it means that their land flowed with milk and honey."' As Dube comments: 'this reading is a subversive post-colonial reading; it invalidates the imperial strategies that employ the rhetoric of poverty and lack of faith among the colonized to justify dominating other nations' ('Readings of *Semoya*', p. 125).

This inclusiveness is shown in the readers' own willingness to borrow from traditions outside Christianity to make the story their own. The very concept of Moya is prevalent in African religions as the present activity of God, which 'enters and empowers women and men'. This taking up of a concept found in both religious traditions is 'both a strategy of resistance and healing from imperial cultural forces of imposition, which depends on devaluing difference and imposing a few universal standards' ('Readings of *Semoya*', p. 125). At the same time the emphasis on the Spirit allows great freedom: members of the Church can speak in the Spirit without other authorization, official or biblical, and this is profoundly liberating for women, who play an important part in the life of the AICs.

Finally, Dube notes that the emphasis on healing is central to the AICs' understanding of their faith. Healing activities of many kinds form a central part of their church life and are open to all. They embrace all aspects of life: 'unemployment, breakdown of relationships, bad harvests, lost cows, evil spirits, bodily illness, and misfortune. . . . Through their claim that God's Spirit empowers them to heal these social ills, AICs join hands with God in a constant struggle against institutional oppression. They offer the promise and the solution. This space of healing becomes their political discourse of confronting social ills, not as helpless beings who are neglected by God, but as those who are in control and capable of changing their social conditions' ('Readings of *Semoya*', pp. 126–7).

Here healing, a motif prominent in the presentation of Jesus in the Gospels, but largely played down in Western interpretations influenced by the Enlightenment, has been given a central position in the AICs' reception of the narrative. Thus there is twofold resistance to the dominant patterns of interpretation which have been purveyed by the mainstream churches. There is resistance to colonialist readings which have marginalized or excluded the colonized: the Bible is appealed to as liberative, as empowering the poor, as open rather than exclusive, as giving authority to women. And there is an assertion of an alternative cosmology: belief in God's action as Moya and the understanding of the Church as a community able to administer his healing action to all are, as Dube suggests, ways of countering the cruel physical and economic conditions which members of the AICs experience. They provide a framework of interpretation, a set of basic beliefs, in terms of which quite new realizations of the biblical texts can be achieved.

Use and abuse

The history of colonial and post-colonial readings of the Bible provides a powerfully instructive study of its uses and abuses. It shows clearly the immense plasticity and fruitfulness of the biblical texts. They are open to the most diverse readings: the same texts, depending on how they are read, can bring either life or death to the same people. This might be enough to lead some to abandon their use altogether. On the other hand, as Lessing pondered some 250 years ago, rejecting the texts altogether means running the danger of turning one's back on vital resources for living.

Discussions like these bring us face to face with an acute dilemma. Those who can take a distanced look at the history of the conquest of Latin America cannot but be repelled by the uses to which the Bible was put in giving moral and religious support to the appalling treatment of the indigenous people by the conquistadores. Nor can we simply dismiss their readings of the Bible as entirely arbitrary: the stories of the massacres of the indigenous people of the land of Canaan in the Bible are equally repugnant. On the other hand, we have strong contemporary evidence that the Bible *can* bring comfort, strength, and liberation to people living under oppression, just as elsewhere it has enriched the culture of both Jews and Christians. There is too much that we should lose, if we were to turn our backs on it, dangerous as it is.

But how to use it? In the first place, critically. We need to be aware both of the different voices in the Bible and of the different ways in which it can be read. We need to learn to discriminate between these different voices and readings and to exercise our own moral judgement. Secondly, we should read charitably. We need to allow the creative, liberative, and constructive voices in the Bible to shape our understanding of the text, rather in the manner in which Desmond Tutu was able to draw together such elements to form a lens through which to view the Bible and also the situation of apartheid South Africa. We should not allow our own moral judgement to be overwhelmed by the darker side of the Bible. However, a critical and attentive reading of the Bible can inform and sharpen our moral sense and provide a moral and religious vision which can transform individuals and communities.

Chapter 9
The Bible in politics

The narratives, laws, and prophecies of the Old Testament/Hebrew Bible make at least one thing clear: God's will and instruction to his people embraced the whole of life. What the people did under leaders like Moses and Aaron, or under the later kings, was a matter to be judged by the Law of God. They owed their existence as a people to God; if they kept his Law he would protect and care for them; when they abandoned it, he would bring judgement, exile, and slavery on them.

The New Testament carries a less clear message: its major figure, Jesus, advocates an ethic which to some has seemed unworldly or utopian. Some of Jesus's sayings can be taken to make a sharp separation between the worldly and the religious sphere: 'Give therefore to the emperor the things that are the emperor's, and to God the things that are God's' (Matthew 22:21); 'My kingdom is not from this world' (John 18:36). Similarly, Paul encourages his Roman correspondents to obey the powers that be (Romans 13:1), while looking for a radical transformation of society where the distinctions between Jew and Gentile, slave and free, male and female, on which Roman society was built will be rolled away (Galatians 3:28). In the book of Revelation Rome is portrayed as the whore of Babylon and the seer looks to its destruction and the time when God's rule will extend over the whole world (Revelation 17:1–6). Sometimes, it seems, the New Testament sets out the

Box 4

'I am puzzled about which Bible people are reading when they suggest religion and politics don't mix.'

Desmond Tutu, Christian Aid poster

ethics for a world which will come into being only when the present rulers of the world have been swept aside and a new heaven and new earth established; at others it seems more concerned to allow the secular world to have its own—independent—sphere of operation, while itself focusing on the affairs of the heavenly kingdom (Box 4).

Given that the biblical texts contain such a complex and in part contradictory message, we may expect their use and impact in shaping the societies in which their interpreters lived to have been similarly diverse. Luther encouraged his followers to live out their faith in their everyday lives and callings, but he also distinguished the kingdom of God from the kingdom of the world in ways which left his followers not always clear where their allegiance to each kingdom might lie. Colonial readings justified the conquest by Christians of lands in Latin America and Africa, the subjugation of indigenous people, and even their extermination. On the other hand, the same Bible could also be a powerful instrument for the liberation of colonized peoples. In this chapter we shall look at some other areas of political life where the Bible has been influential in forming political doctrines and practice, though not always without opposition.

Allegiance to the state: oaths and arms-bearing

Not all the Reformers were happy with Luther's sharp division between the worldly and the spiritual kingdoms. The Anabaptists and others in the Radical Reformation tradition quite soon abandoned the attempt to find some way of working with secular rulers and formed distinct communities of their own, where all members were committed to living out the Sermon on the Mount. They avoided ostentatious clothing and wealth and refused to swear oaths in court, to bear arms, or to defend themselves. Those who found the administration of oaths and capital punishment, 'the power of the sword', to be a necessary means of maintaining law and order saw in these ardent advocates of an evangelical ethic a dire threat to civil stability and dealt with them fiercely.

The Quakers in England, like the Anabaptists, interpreted the commandments of the Sermon of the Mount literally and so refused to bear arms or to swear oaths. They met with fierce opposition and many left to find a new life in the New World. Life in the English colonies proved little better and Quakers who had arrived in Massachusetts in 1657 were flogged, and had their ears cropped. Four were hanged for missionary activity. Remarkably, in 1682, a prominent Quaker in England, William Penn, who had been imprisoned in the Tower for his beliefs but who had strong family connections with the future James II, was granted a royal charter for a new colony, in an area embracing present-day Pennsylvania and Delaware. His new colony, which included previous Dutch and Swedish settlers, rejected the use of coercion in religion, welcomed all monotheists of whatever persuasion, and sought friendly relations with native Americans. It soon attracted a wide range of English, Scots, and continental European Protestants, including members of many of the Radical Reformation groups.

The Quaker preacher George Fox's position on oaths was clear: 'Take heed of giving people oaths to swear, for Christ our Lord and master saith, "Swear not at all; but let your communication be yea, yea, and nay, nay: for whatsoever is more than these cometh of evil."' What gave truth to all and made them testify to it was the 'light in every man'; oaths and swearing were but 'idle words' for which men would answer on judgement day (Boorstin,

The Americans, p. 44). The Old Testament rules for swearing oaths were specifically for the Jews and could not stand against the words of Jesus and James, who had forbidden all swearing. Fox had been brought to court in 1656 for advocating such views, but by 1689 Quakers were permitted to make a simple affirmation 'in the presence of Almighty God' and at the same time excluded from giving evidence in criminal cases, serving as jurors, and holding public office.

In Pennsylvania, a law allowed people to give witness by 'solemnly promising to speak the truth, the whole truth and nothing but the truth'. But there were problems. Pennsylvania was an English colony and conflict with English law was possible. Further, many settlers were uneasy with witnesses and jurors who would not take traditional oaths. Finally, a compromise was reached. The Crown agreed that Quakers themselves might make the affirmation in criminal cases and as office-holders without any reference to God, but insisted that others should take oaths administered to them by the appropriate officials. This had the effect, since Quakers would also not administer oaths, of excluding Quakers from certain public offices, most significantly those of magistrates and judges.

More serious tests were to come over the question of arms-bearing. Quakers were committed to pacifism. George Fox had refused to fight for the commonwealth against Charles Stuart. His position was firmly based on biblical texts:

> 'We are peaceable, and seek the peace, good and welfare of all... For Christ said, "His Kingdom was not of this world, if it were his servants would fight." Therefore he bid Peter, "put up his sword; for", said he, "he that taketh the sword shall perish by the sword." Here is the faith and patience of the saints, to bear and suffer all things, knowing vengeance is the Lord's, and he will repay to them that hurt his people and wrong the innocent; therefore cannot we avenge but suffer for his name's sake.'
>
> (Boorstin, *The Americans*, pp. 48–9)

Quakers might have hoped that they had escaped from England to a land where they would be free to pursue a peaceable way of life, free from the military and political ambitions of the British Crown, but Pennsylvania's status as a colony made this impossible. They were involved in a series of wars against the French and the Spanish, but largely protected from the king's enemies by the colonies to the north and the south. Later, however, they experienced attacks from the Native Americans who were being squeezed by the warring colonists. In 1755 settlers on the western frontier suffered terribly at their hands and Franklin, then the leader of a compromise party in the Assembly, mobilized opinion in favour of raising the necessary military forces to defend the colony. In 1756 the governor and the council declared war on the Delaware and Shewanee Indians. The Quaker majority in the Pennsylvania Assembly resigned.

There are those like the American historian Daniel Boorstin who lament the Quakers' concern with the purity of their own motives and actions. Had they had been willing to compromise, they could have held on to power and exerted a greater influence on the subsequent development of society in the United States. But it is hard to know where one can compromise as a pacifist without ceasing to be true to one's principles. Their fellow Quakers in England urged them not to waver. They were a peaceable people. If they should ever take up arms, they would lose their identity and cease to bear witness to the truth. They had set out to build a society where such principles would be followed as public policy. However, their affairs were never exclusively in their own hands, as the controversies over oath-swearing make clear. What went on in Pennsylvania was caught up in British imperial ambitions; others who came to live in the colony might have rather different understandings of the way to deal with those who pillaged their settlements. Quakers, in their attempts to make their principles into public policy, were unable to deal with the need to balance different and inevitably conflicting principles. And so they became a marginal but prophetic group willing to testify with their lives to the atrocity of war and coercion. This may not lead to long-lasting polities, such as those which Luther's doctrines spawned. It may, however, precisely by refusing to abandon the claim that such principles should have a bearing on public life, have a lasting contribution to make, which is not possible for those who make a sharp separation between the ethics of the spiritual and the worldly kingdoms.

Gender politics

The story of the struggles of the Quakers in Pennsylvania to build a society based on pacifist principles makes clear how great the challenges are which face those who seek to follow some of the principles and precepts in the New Testament. They can seem so radically opposed to firmly entrenched practices in—all?—societies (including those which have drawn heavily on other aspects of the Bible) that they can at best be lived out in alternative societies, separated as far as possible from mainstream society. Paul's statement in Galatians 3:28 that in Christ there is neither Jew nor Gentile, slave nor free, male nor female, sets out a vision of a world built on radically different foundations from those which upheld 1st-century society and, indeed many others. And yet there have been those who have found in such texts the inspiration to challenge such deep-seated beliefs and practice and to shake the foundations of the worlds they inhabited. So let us consider one of the issues raised here, that of male/female relationships.

There is no doubting the radical nature of Paul's claim that in Christ there is neither male nor female. The Bible itself has been a major source of the patriarchy which has marked Christian societies, commanding women to be submissive to men and exalting maleness over femaleness. We noticed earlier the attitudes to women in the two creation narratives. The New Testament contains injunctions to women to be silent in church (1 Corinthians 14:34) and to wives to be submissive to their husbands in all things (Ephesians 5:21–33). Such sayings have been taken up and incorporated into the life of the churches over the centuries to the point where, with the rise of feminism, many women have felt that there is no longer any place for them in mainstream churches. Others, however, still believe that there are resources within the churches and the Bible which are liberating and can lead the Church and society to embrace more egalitarian, less hierarchical forms of association. How do they proceed?

In the first instance, commentators like the American Old Testament scholar Phyllis Trible have worked, with great passion, to raise people's awareness of the oppressiveness of many of the biblical narratives. In her *Texts of Terror*, she brings out the terrifying nature of the way in which women are treated in some of them. In Judges 11, Jephthah vows to God that he will sacrifice the first person that he meets coming out of his house on his return from battle, if he is successful. The fact that it is his daughter does not deter him from keeping his vow. And there is much more of this kind, some of which we will consider when reviewing Margaret Atwood's *The Handmaid's Tale* in Chapter 10.

Such a consciousness-raising exercise is necessary if the Bible is to be made use of at all in attempting to find alternatives to patriarchy. But what positive resources does it offer? Let me consider two rather different, though complementary, approaches to this question. Elisabeth Schüssler-Fiorenza, a New Testament scholar teaching in the United States, has sought in her work to rewrite the history of early Christianity to show the importance within it of egalitarian traditions stemming from Jesus. Jesus in his preaching of the kingdom proclaims that salvation is dawning. The reality of this new salvation is symbolized in his meals: 'It is the festive table-sharing at a wedding-feast, and not the askesis of the "holy man", that characterizes Jesus and his movement… Not the holiness of the elect, but the wholeness *of all* is the central vision of Jesus' (Schüssler-Fiorenza, *In Memory of Her*, pp. 119, 121). All are included, '[w]omen as well as men, prostitutes as well as Pharisees'. Jesus's vision is therefore opposed to patriarchy, to any attempt to divide the united community, to set one section against another. Galatians 3:28 is a key text for Schüssler-Fiorenza, but also important are the Gospel traditions which set aside patriarchal family relationships in favour of the 'discipleship of equals' of those who 'do the will of God': they are the ones who are to be called 'my brother, and sister, and mother' (Mark 3:35). Thus all titles and hierarchical distinctions are to be set aside: 'And call no one your father on earth, for you have one Father-who is in heaven. Nor are you to be called instructors, for you have one instructor, the Messiah' (Matthew 23:9–10) (Schüssler-Fiorenza, *Discipleship of Equals*, pp. 176–7). And, she argues, this egalitarian ethos is reflected in the history of the early Christian mission, in which women played a full role alongside men.

Yet while there is clear evidence within the New Testament of a 'discipleship of equals', with women playing an important part in key events, remaining at the cross, being primary witnesses to the Resurrection (John 20:11–18), there is also evidence of resistance to such egalitarianism. Whereas Paul in 1 Corinthians 15:5–8 has a wide list of those who can operate as authoritative witnesses to Jesus's death and resurrection (although even here there is no explicit mention of women), Luke's Gospel, often thought of as being the most sympathetic to women, excludes women from the witnesses to the resurrection: the apostles alone, foremost among them Peter, see the risen Jesus. Schüssler-Fiorenza believes that this emphasis on Peter must 'be situated within the early Christian discussion of whether Peter or Mary of Magdala qualifies as the first resurrection witness' (*Discipleship of Equals*, p. 164). More widely, one can discern a tendency to suppress evidence of the role of women in the earliest Christian communities, and the growing patriarchalization of the community in the second and third generations.

Schüssler-Fiorenza describes her work in *In Memory of Her* as a 'feminist theological reconstruction of Christian origins'. It is an attempt to recover a history of Christian origins which has been obscured, partly by patriarchal tendencies within the New Testament itself, partly by the subsequent historiography of the Church. Such a reconstruction is theological in that it looks for the key theological vision of Jesus and the early Christians; it is feminist in that its critical reading of the New Testament texts is informed and impelled by the experience of 'women's struggle for liberation from oppression' (*In Memory of Her*, p. 32). It treats the New Testament, or rather the picture of the Church that it presents, not as a timeless archetype of the ideal form of church life, but as a prototype 'which is critically open to the possibility of its own transformation' (p. 33).

Other feminist writers treat the Bible and its stories, images, and metaphors, alongside women's writing of all kinds, as imaginative resources for the refashioning of the Church's traditions. Mary Grey, an English Catholic theologian, in *Beyond the Dark Night*, deploys a whole cluster of images in an attempt to conjure up the new form of the Church which will emerge in and through its 'dark night'. In a chapter on journeying, she explores the 'condensed symbol of exodus from oppression, wandering in the wilderness—while experiencing the presence of God in a way—and hoping for the Promised Land' (p. 48). Use of such symbols of the 'creative imagination is a key tool in journeying from alienated forms of Christian living'. Images of the Exodus, which were so important an inspiration for liberation theology, no longer provide spiritual dynamism to those in former communist countries who are now themselves suffering in their new life within the capitalist fold. 'The vision of the socialist Utopia had vanished, and what remained were the seductive arms of capitalism. Wandering in the wilderness without vision summed up their situation symbolically' (p. 48). In such situations, images of exile may exert a more powerful attraction. What Mary Grey advocates is not exodus from the Church, but the refocusing of symbols of exodus as symbols of exodus from 'alienated relationships'.

> A sacramental life which alienates large categories of believers from the table of the eucharist is in danger of being alienated sacramental life...A theology of sexuality which condemns to the status of deviants...a large proportion of human beings is alienated sexuality. Understandings of power, priesthood, and authority which reduce the pilgrim people to disempowerment and passivity are alienated understandings. (p. 50)

Here biblical imagery is contextualized: the images and symbolism of the Bible are drawn on freely in a search for wholeness and inclusion in the face of alienating forces in Church and community, which threaten to stifle and break human relationships. The Bible is not appealed to as a set of norms, but drawn on, freely and selectively, as a resource of imagery which can give shape and form to people's life experiences.

The Bible as political authority

This has been a very partial survey of the uses of the Bible in politics. It would have been possible to include many other issues in public policy: welfare, slavery, economics, genetics, medicine, and so on. Given the enormous status and authority of the Bible in Europe throughout most of the last 2,000 years, this is hardly surprising. Politicians would hardly be politicians if they were to ignore potential sources of ideological support—or indeed opposition.

Even in such a survey it is difficult not to be struck by the conflicting ways in which the Bible has been used. Luther and the mainstream Reformers used it to justify the power of the sword and to draw a clear line between the laws which were to govern secular society and the teaching of the Sermon on the Mount which was intended only for Christians. Those who on the other hand insisted that Jesus's teachings should be put into practice in the life of the state had then to face the practical difficulties of embodying statements of great generality in institutions and legislation for very particular communities facing quite specific situations and dangers. Both sides of this debate, however, were agreed in seeing the Bible as a book with a coherent message for Church and society, however much they might disagree about the nature of that message. The feminist critics we have looked at are much clearer that there is plenty in the Bible which is unacceptable and that the real struggle is to discern those elements which could provide resources in the search for a new Church and a new society. Here the process of discernment is ultimately to be governed by the experience of women's struggles. But equally, different strategies can be devised for separating the more creative resources out from the rest. For some, historical criticism could enable them to discern elements in the tradition almost obscured by subsequent ideological bias. For others, it is the recontextualizing of biblical imagery and symbolism which can assist the imaginative leap whereby new forms of life and community can emerge out of the biblical traditions. To return to earlier discussions, we may see at work here two rather different conceptions of the canon. For the first, the canon is still seen as normative, although it is a norm which has first to be established by historical discernment of the truly binding elements within the texts. For the latter, the canonical authority of the Bible is first and foremost formative: it provides the tools and imagery which can both enslave and liberate. Discernment is just as necessary: however, the test is practical rather than historical.

Chapter 10
The Bible in high and popular culture

The Bible is one of the main sources of European culture. In its various translations, it has had a formative influence on the language, the literature, the art, the music of all the major European and North American cultures. It continues to influence popular culture in films, novels, and music. Its language, stories, metaphors, types, and figures provide a vast cultural resource which is drawn on in a bewildering variety of ways, both consciously and unconsciously. From elaborate retellings of the narratives in great novels like Thomas Mann's *Joseph and his Brothers* and in musical representation like Bach's *St Matthew Passion,* through Rembrandt's intimate depictions of biblical scenes and narratives, to echoes of biblical metaphor and motifs in poetry and fiction, there is a huge range of use. Poets like Milton and Blake must remain largely unintelligible to those without a knowledge of their biblical sources; in other writers it is more as if they are drawing on some 'great code' which is so much part of the cultural heritage that it is almost impossible to escape from it, whether one is conscious of its biblical origins or not.

Biblical retellings: the Bible in music

The retelling of biblical narratives is a feature of the Bible itself. The stories of the books of Kings are repeated in the books of

Chronicles; the Gospel story is retold three times. Moreover, as we have already seen, this tradition of retelling appears in Jewish and Christian writing from as early as the 2nd century BCE. The story of Abraham's binding of Isaac is retold in the book of Jubilees, in Josephus' *Antiquities*, in Midrash, and in the poetry of the Middle Ages. Such retellings helped hearers make sense of their own experience; they also served to inscribe their experience in their canonical texts. Such reciprocity—the use of the cultural language of the Bible to make sense of new and often disturbing experience and the reshaping/rereading of the canonical texts in the light of such bewildering and anomalous experience—would encourage writers, artists, and musicians to continue this tradition outside the confines of the community of faith.

The development of such retelling of the biblical narratives outside a specific church context must have been gradual. The medieval Passion plays are a good example of the way in which the telling of the story spills out of the church confines onto a wider stage. The story of the Oberammergau Passion play, which originated as a thanksgiving for deliverance from the plague, indicates how such popular re-enactments of the Passion may have a very specific reference to events in the community's history. Such plays are expansions of the medieval liturgical practice of reading or chanting the Gospel Passion narratives in dramatized form—different voices representing the evangelist, the various characters, and the crowd. This musical tradition was developed in the 17th century with the emergence of opera, oratorio, and cantata and their attendant forms of aria, recitative, and chorale. New texts for the arias and chorales were added to the text of the Gospel making it possible to give greater expression to the emotions of the participants. By the beginning of the 18th century this tendency had gone so far that Passions were written which no longer adhered to the text of the Gospels but were a complete retelling. Bach's two surviving Passions, the *St John Passion* and the *St Matthew Passion*, still retained the medieval practice of presenting the full text of the Gospel, though in the *St John Passion* Bach added passages from Matthew's Gospel (the evangelist's comment after the cockcrow and the earthquake after Jesus's death) to provide additional colour.

Overall the earlier *St John Passion* is sparer; the text of the Gospel stands out more clearly. Even so, the music clearly underlines certain themes. In the first place, the choir's parts in the Gospel, which provide a wonderful opportunity for Bach to display his dramatic skills, underline the way in which Jesus is abandoned by his own people, as first the high priests and their servants and then 'the Jews' cry out for his crucifixion.

Between them, however, Bach sets a chorale:

> Through your prison, Son of God,
> Freedom has come to us.
> Your dungeon is the throne of grace,
> The place of deliverance for all the faithful.
> If you had not taken slavery upon yourself, our slavery would be eternal.

The effect of this is twofold: in the first place there can be no denying the way in which the opposition of the Jews and their part in Jesus's condemnation to death is emphasized. This is certainly an emphasis in the Gospel text, but the gusto with which the choir calls for his crucifixion underlines their participation. Nevertheless it is not the centrepiece: this is provided by the chorale. Here Lutheran notions of Christ's paying the penalty for human sin, of humanity as weighed down by the burden of its guilt, are central. The focus of the Passion is on humanity's struggle for peace and freedom from guilt. But the musical force of the presentation of the Jewish crowds remains and is intensified in the later *St Matthew Passion*, which also develops the arias and chorales in the same Lutheran direction.

Bach's Passions were originally written for the Lutheran observance of Holy Week in Leipzig in the first part of the 18th century. They still remain a firm part of Lutheran observance (though now rarely given as part of a church service) but have also made their way effortlessly into the concert hall. This ability of liturgical works to transfer into a secular context is testimony to the way in which great liturgical compositions address and enable the participants to confront the *grandeurs et misères* of human existence.

A similar expansion of liturgical form occurs in Britten's *War Requiem* (see Figure 6) where the composer incorporates the First World War poems of Wilfred Owen into the text of the Requiem Mass. At the offertory, where the elements of bread and wine are presented for the sacrifice of the mass, the boys' choir prays for deliverance for the souls of the faithful from the pains of hell and that Michael might lead them into holy light 'which, of old, Thou didst promise unto Abraham and his seed'. This last phrase is taken up in an extended fugue which leads into Owen's reworking of the Akedah narrative:

> So Abram rose, and clave the wood, and went,
> And took the fire with him, and a knife.
> And as they sojourned both of them together,
> Isaac the first-born spake and said, My Father,
> Behold the preparations, fire and iron,
> But where the lamb for this burnt-offering?
> Then Abram bound the youth with belts and straps,
> And builded parapets and trenches there,
> And stretched forth the knife to slay his son.
> When lo! an angel called him out of heav'n,
> Saying, Lay not thy hand upon the lad,
> Neither do anything to him. Behold,
> A ram, caught in a thicket by its horns;
> Offer the Ram of Pride instead of him.
> But the old man would not so, but slew his son,—
> And half the seed of Europe, one by one.

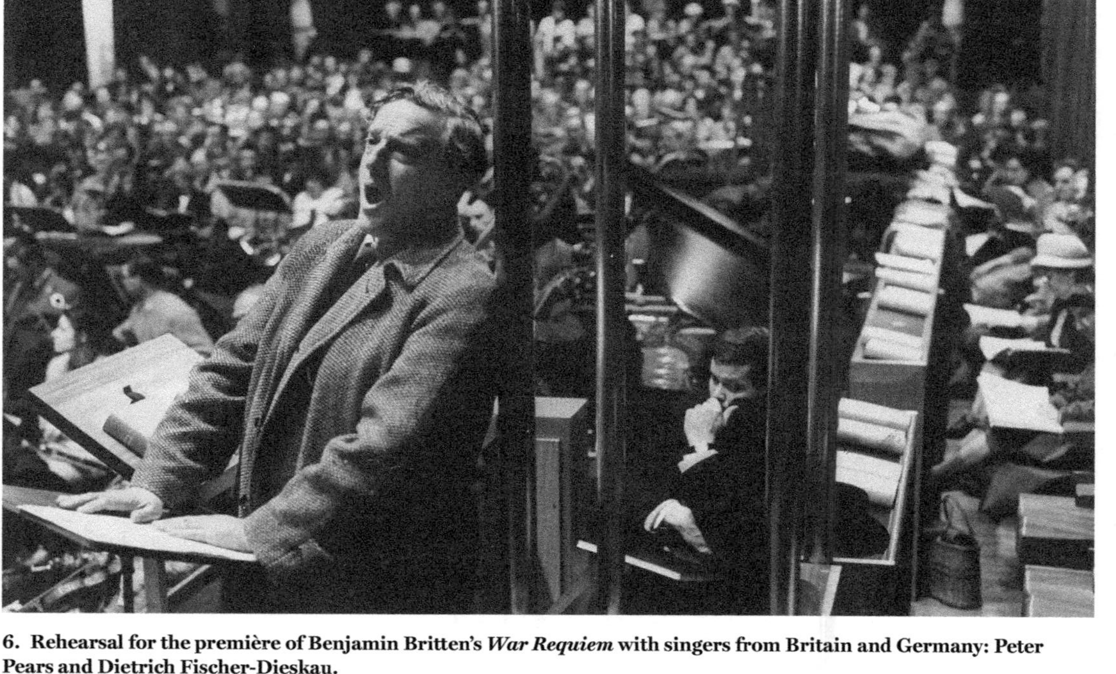

6. Rehearsal for the première of Benjamin Britten's *War Requiem* with singers from Britain and Germany: Peter Pears and Dietrich Fischer-Dieskau.

As the soloists repeat the last line of the poem, the boys' chorus enters again with the words of the offertory and its reference to the promises to Abraham and his seed.

As in Rabbi Ephraim's poem (see Chapter 5), the story is broken under the weight of the poet's suffering. But the rabbi's poem, even though Isaac dies, still ends with his resurrection and the vindication of Abraham's faith. Owen's 'old man' slays the seed of Europe 'one by one' on the parapets of the trenches, refusing to accept the Ram of Pride for his sacrifice. In Britten's setting the voices of the soldiers are accompanied by the choirs pleading for the resurrection of the slain: 'make them, O Lord, to pass from death unto life, which thou didst promise to Abraham and his seed'. By comparison with the rabbi's poem, there is here a far more violent rupture between the retelling and its original. The very ground of the story—Abraham's faith in God who will preserve him and his forebears—is questioned by the action of Abraham towards his own son. The son's question 'My Father...' is repeated by the tenor and contrasts the son's innocent trust with the senseless slaughter that follows. There is no looking back to the inherited, archetypal faith of Abraham: only the image of the damaged wayside crucifix, of the crucified deserted by his followers but with the soldiers clustered round, offers any hope:

> One ever hangs where shelled roads part.
> In this war He too lost a limb,
> But now His disciples hide apart;
> And the soldiers bear with him.

Owen's poem is interspersed with the Latin text of the Agnus Dei: O Lamb of God, Who takest away the sins of the world, grant them rest. The effect of his reworking of the Abraham story is to force a re-evaluation of the tradition: to challenge the priests and scribes who have been corrupted by national pride and unquestioning obedience to the state. The slain lamb replaces the Ram of Pride.

Biblical images in art

Although the Bible consists solely of written material, it has spawned a whole world of imagery and pictorial art. Again, this starts within the worshipping communities of the Bible, more so among Christians than Jews, who were far more cautious about the use of images in their synagogues. Church iconography, paintings, mosaics, frescos, and stained-glass windows, decorated and instructed at the same time: the Bible of the poor. The great Italian masters like Michelangelo in the Sistine Chapel (1508–13, see Figure 7) and Giotto in the Scrovegni Chapel in Padua (*c.*1305, see Figure 8) worked to a grand scheme.

Giotto's frescos run in four bands along facing walls of the chapel, depicting (from top to bottom) scenes from the life of Mary, scenes from the life of Christ, and allegorizations of virtues and vices. On the triumphal arch leading into the sanctuary there is a depiction of the Annunciation, on the west wall a portrayal of the Last Judgement. As in the Sistine Chapel, the pictures are there not only to remind the congregation of the individual stories from the Bible. They are by no means all biblical. Their role is to present a comprehensive world-view, concentrated on redemption through the incarnation, with its preparation in the life of the Virgin. The personal implications of such a view of the world are made plain in the panels depicting the vices and the virtues and in the stark contrasts of the Last Judgement. In later Renaissance art such schemes are expanded and scenes from the Old Testament are compared and contrasted typologically with those of the New.

For all the tenderness and humanity of Giotto's depiction of the New Testament characters, his work remains in a sense schematic, presenting the official doctrine of the Church in a set format. The art of the Renaissance introduces a more individualistic, more personal element into its depiction of biblical scenes. Donatello's wonderful bronze of David (*c.*1446–60) is a study of boyish beauty

7. Michelangelo's depiction of the *Final Judgement* in the Sistine Chapel in the Vatican, Rome.

and introspection; Masaccio's depiction of the expulsion of Adam and Eve from the Garden, in the Brancacci chapel in Florence (*c.*1425), is an extraordinary study of human desolation and loss. A century later Grünewald, in his Isenheim altar (*c.*1513–15), will spare no effort in portraying the physical torture and suffering of

8. One of Giotto's frescos from the Cappella Scrovegni in Padua.

the crucified Jesus. Whereas in the other panels of the altar the angelic, heavenly world hovers in the background or actively intervenes, here all is dark, bereft of the divine glory: it is an extraordinary portrayal of the Son of God's identification with the god-forsakenness of the afflicted.

There is a similarity of theme in Rembrandt's oil *Entombment Sketch* in the Hunterian Art Gallery in Glasgow (see Figure 9). Christ's body is being laid in a tomb cut into the rock, with an entrance to the right. An old man holds his shoulders; the main weight of the shroud in which the body is being lowered is taken by a younger man, behind whom stands a figure supporting himself on the rock; on the right a turbaned, kneeling figure holds the shroud at his ankles. To the left of this group is a woman holding a torch and shielding it with her hand; next to her stands an old bearded man. Behind this main group and to the right there is a further group of figures, dominated by a large figure

9. Rembrandt's *Entombment Sketch* in the Hunterian Art Gallery, Glasgow University.

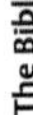

carrying a lantern. A remarkable feature of the painting, for which Rembrandt uses mainly brown, ochre, and white paint, is its use of light and dark: one's eyes have to become accustomed to the subtlety of the play of light, which only just allows the outlines of some of the figures on the right to emerge. By contrast, the light from the body of Christ can be seen from across the gallery.

Rembrandt painted a similar *Entombment*, now in Munich, probably some time before the Glasgow painting. The Munich work forms part of a set of paintings, including an *Adoration of the Shepherds*. Strikingly, the *Adoration of the Shepherds* in Munich closely resembles the Glasgow *Entombment*, both in its composition, which is almost its mirror image, and in the way that the light seems to radiate from the infant Christ. Thus the figures in the Glasgow painting seem to be subtly caught between grief, tenderness, and adoration. Interestingly, Rembrandt overpainted the figure of a prostrate woman at Christ's feet with the present kneeling figure. It seems that he preferred a figure kneeling in adoration to that of one prostrate in grief.

The relation of Rembrandt's painting to the Gospel text is complex. Matthew's account of Jesus's death and burial, in particular, contrasts the dramatic events which accompanied his death—the rending of the Temple veil, an earthquake, with rocks split, tombs opening, and 'saints appearing'—with the entombment and sealing of the tomb with a large rock (Matthew 27:51–4, 59–61).

In a number of paintings, engravings, and sketches one can see Rembrandt working on the details which the text omits: the manner in which the body was taken down from the cross and was carried to the tomb, the scene inside the tomb. In the Munich painting, the eye is led away from the figures in the tomb: through a hole in the rock the crosses can be seen. In the Glasgow painting, by contrast, the entrance is obscured: it is almost as if one were in the sealed tomb. The sealing of the tomb is echoed in the closed-in feeling of the painting. But equally Rembrandt allows the viewer to see what it is that will roll back the stone: the power of the new life which resides in the dead Christ, mourned, cherished, and adored by his few remaining friends and family. Here Rembrandt is indeed an interpreter of his text.

Biblical symbolism: the Bible in metaphor and concept

It is not just in the retelling of the great stories of the Bible, whether in literature, music, pictorial art, or indeed film, that the Bible has shaped and informed the European cultural heritage. In *La Dolce Vita,* Fellini punctuated his account of the decadence of modern Roman society with images and motifs taken from the book of Revelation. Ingmar Bergman's *The Seventh Seal* uses similar motifs in his dark film of the plague. The language, metaphors, and concepts of the Bible permeate our culture in endless kinds of ways: from the turn of phrase which may add a twist to a scene, through the exploitation of major biblical metaphors and concepts which may shape a work as a whole, however they are received or reworked (or indeed rejected), to works which reflect on the role of the Bible itself.

Margaret Atwood's *The Handmaid's Tale* provides a powerful contemporary example. It tells of Gilead, an authoritarian post-nuclear state in North America, where human fertility has dropped alarmingly, and where a class of 'handmaids' has been created, who are allocated to childless couples among the leadership with the specific task of bearing children. They are tightly controlled and subject to fierce punishments and eventual banishment to the colonies or execution if they fail to conceive or if they rebel.

The biblical word 'handmaid' is a convenient euphemism for their enslavement, having its root in the Hebrew *'amah,* meaning maidservant or female slave. The key sense for the novel is given by the reference to the slave girl Bilhah (Genesis 30:1–9), whom Rachel gives to Jacob, out of her jealousy for her sister Leah's success in childbearing. This is what Offred, the narrator of the tale, refers to as 'the mouldy old Rachel and Leah stuff we had drummed into us at the Centre' (*The Handmaid's Tale*, p. 99). It also resonates with the story of Abraham, Sarah, and Hagar. Hagar is the slave given to Abraham when Sarah fails to conceive, who is subsequently driven out into the desert with her son when Sarah succeeds (Genesis 21:8–21). Perhaps most significantly, it echoes Mary's words at the Annunciation, 'Behold the handmaid of the Lord; be it unto me according to thy word' (Luke 1:38). In short, the term is connected with slavery, sexual exploitation, and submissiveness.

However, there is another, more subversive strand of narrative which is linked to the use of the term 'handmaid' in the Bible, which embraces figures like Abigail (1 Samuel 25), who averts the threat of the destruction of her people by running to David from her husband Nabal, a series of 'wise-women' who advise the Jewish kings, and finally Judith, who tricks the Assyrian general Holofernes when she offers to tell the Assyrians a secret way into the city of Bethulia, gets him drunk, and cuts his head off with his own sword (Judith 13:4). The story is reminiscent of an earlier killing of a foreign invader, Sisera. Here Jael, the wife of Heber, takes the fleeing general into her tent and drives a tent peg through his temples (Judges 4:22).

This too finds its echoes in the tale. Offred, after she has kissed the Commander in his room (something strictly forbidden), contemplates removing the lever from the toilet cistern and then 'driv[ing] the sharp end into him, suddenly, between his ribs. I think about the blood coming out of him, hot as soup, sexual, over my hands' (*The Handmaid's Tale*, p. 150, see Figure 10). Thus the tale picks up age-old themes about the struggle of women against

10. Dangerous encounter between the Commander and Offred in *The Handmaid's Tale*.

men's domination and overarches the present by setting them in a putative future world.

The book also comments directly on the Bible's role in all this. The Commander reads carefully selected and bookmarked passages from the Bible to the household.

> The Bible is kept locked up, so the servants won't steal it. It is an incendiary device: who knows what we'd make of it, if we ever got our hands on it? We can be read from it, by him, but we cannot read. Our heads turn towards him, we are expectant, here comes our bedtime story.... the usual story, the usual stories. God to Adam, God to Noah. Be fruitful, and multiply, and replenish the earth. Then comes the mouldy old Rachel and Leah stuff.
>
> (*The Handmaid's Tale*, pp. 97–9)

Atwood's portrayal of the use of the canon to control a totalitarian society is full of subtlety. In *The Handmaid's Tale*, and its sequel, *The Testaments*, she shows how tightly managed the Bible must be if it is to be read normatively to support specific rules and practices. Only selected passages, suitably interpreted, can be used. When Agnes, in *The Testaments* (pp. 302–3), gets access to the full text of the Bible and can see 'what had been changed by Gilead, what had been added, and what had been omitted', her faith in Gilead is threatened. Uncontrolled, unexpurgated, the Bible is unpredictable, dangerous, 'incendiary'.

The root of culture

This chapter can give only a brief impression of the sheer fecundity of the Bible, its ability to inspire an immense variety of cultural expressions, of the many things, good and bad, that people can make of it, 'once they get their hands on it'. Part of the problem for our society lies in its widespread ignorance of the Bible. The handmaids in Atwood's tale know only what they are told and are unaware of its subversive capabilities. To the extent that we are not even aware of those themes and motifs from the Bible which hold us and condition our social mores, our position may be even worse. For how then can we criticize, let alone recover the biblical elements in our culture? The way to a deeper appreciation and critique of our cultural heritage is barred. So too is the way to a more liberating and redemptive use of the Bible.

Chapter 11
Conclusion

I hope this brief survey of the Bible and its uses has shown something of the richness of the ways in which it has been read and appropriated. It has provided a source of religious and moral norms which have enabled communities to hold together, to care for, and to protect one another; yet precisely this strong sense of belonging has in turn fuelled ethnic, racial, and international tension and conflict. It has inspired some of the great monuments of human thought, literature, and art; it has equally fuelled some of the worst excesses of human savagery, self-interest, and narrow-mindedness. It has inspired men and women to acts of great service and courage, to fight for liberation and human development; and it has provided the ideological fuel for societies which have enslaved their fellow human beings and reduced them to abject poverty. It has been at the root of the great revivals of Christianity, most recently in its remarkable growth in Africa and Asia.

It has, that is to say, been the source of great truth, goodness, and beauty at the same time as it has inspired lies, wickedness, and ugliness. What it has not produced is a uniform manner of its reading and interpretation. The reason for this is simple: texts have no control over the way they are read. 'Texts,' wrote Robert Morgan, 'like dead men, have no rights' (*Biblical Interpretation*, p. 7). It is the reader or communities of readers who produce the readings. And the diversity of readings produced is in proportion to the diversity of reading communities.

Such diversity should not, however, be attributed solely to the diversity of readers. The sheer richness of material in the Bible, the complexity of the processes whereby its books came to be written, the profusion of metaphor, of poetry, of narrative and discourse, would hardly lead us to expect that this collection of books would receive a single uncontroversial reading. At all times and in all places its many readers have had plenty to choose from, every opportunity to emphasize different aspects.

This diversity of material within the Bible has of course been a source of concern for leaders of religious communities, who have seen in their sacred writings a source of religious and moral norms, of revealed truth. The very process of canonization, of establishing an agreed list of books which are recognized as authoritative and excluding others which are not, is part of an attempt to limit diversity and deviance of belief within the community. Within Christianity, the creation of a second canon of New Testament scripture represents a further attempt to determine and limit the ways in which scripture is read: the Old is to be read through the lens of the New; but equally the New will receive a particular set of meanings from being linked with the Old.

Furthermore, once the boundaries of the canon are set, the books within it can never be read in quite the same way again, at least within those communities which accept them as canonical. For they have now become part of an authoritative corpus: they have been declared to be the word of God and there must then be limits to the diversity of viewpoint which can be tolerated among them. Once texts are canonized, the believers' expectations of them soar. Readers have to read them according to a 'principle of charity' whereby they are read not only in such a way as to make sense (even though parts of them may appear obscure and incomprehensible), but also in such a way as to explain apparent or real contradictions and to rework the meaning of passages that may otherwise seem to contradict the teachings of the authorizing body.

But the fact is that canonization of sacred writings is a very rough tool for dealing with religious deviance. The sheer diversity of Protestant churches, all of which recognize the same canon, is ample proof of this. If there is to be a measure of consistency in scriptural interpretation within a given community and hence a measure of stability within that community, further strategies will be needed. This may be achieved in different ways. In the first place, access to the sacred books may be restricted. Only readers who have the required skills and qualifications for interpreting them in ways which will ensure uniformity and continuity of interpretation will be admitted. Within Judaism, this role falls to the scholar/rabbi. Within Christianity, it falls to the clergy, acting under the authority of the bishops or other kinds of church leaders.

The task of these interpreters is partly to lay down the rules of interpretation, partly to construe the texts in such a way that they do indeed offer a reading which is self-consistent and consistent with the norms of the community. With a collection of sacred texts as diverse as those contained in the Bible this will entail not only devising strategies for accommodating passages whose most evident sense is in flagrant contradiction to the central beliefs of the community; it will also entail setting emphases—highlighting certain texts and relegating others to relative insignificance. Crucially, it will entail devising techniques, such as allegory, whereby alternative meanings can be imparted to texts whose literal sense is either unedifying or simply in conflict with the rule of faith of the community. The history of interpretation of the Bible provides rich pickings for those who look for examples of interpretative dexterity and imagination.

Within such rules and interpretative practices, there is then room for a controlled diversity of reading. Interpreters can relate the texts to the experience of their readers and indeed, as we have seen, allow such experience to affect their retelling of the text. There is room for debate and controversy, and there is the stuff of real division. The medieval Church managed to contain diversity of interpretation by a mixture of high-level control—theological and political—and permitted diversity of theologies, forms of life, and religious orders. It also relied on ruthless suppression or marginalization of those whom it deemed deviants, such as Jews, Cathars, and Hussites. It certainly produced its share of deviants, among them the Augustinian friar who would destroy its unity, Martin Luther.

Luther's attack on the sacramental order of the Church, with its clerical monopoly on the dispensing of grace, was altogether an attack from within. It was based on his interpretation of the Pauline texts about justification by faith. It relied on a strictly grammatical reading of these texts, something which was entirely permissible under the existing rules and practices of interpretation in the late medieval Church. Luther himself was an accredited teacher of the Bible. In normal circumstances such anomalous behaviour could have been dealt with internally too. A number of factors made his attack fatal, not the least of which was the invention of the printing press, which enabled his views to be rapidly and widely disseminated. At the same time his (and others') translations of the Bible into the vernacular provided wide popular access to the texts which till then had been largely the preserve of the clergy. The clerical monopoly was broken; from now on every man and woman could be their own interpreter.

The subsequent explosion of new readings of the Bible, of new forms of religious devotion and ways of life, is hardly adequately described as a reformation. The Reformers may indeed have seen it in just those terms: returning to the true form of the Church as revealed in scripture to those who would read and follow its plain, literal sense. In practice what happened was much more like the opening of Pandora's box: once the winds were out, there was no way of putting them back. Older readings of scripture would continue to have their place alongside a whole variety of new ones. New religious communities would spring up all over Europe and from there spread out all over the globe. It was a time of great renewal and life, which in turn provoked fierce conflict and recrimination. Nearly a third of the population of Europe died in the conflagration of the religious wars in the first half of the 16th century. Yet even beyond such conflict the Bible has continued to provide communities with a basis for living and has, as we have seen, taken root in communities all over the globe, even among peoples who have experienced abuse in its name. Diversity of readings, it seems, is here to stay (Box 5).

Of course, there are still those who believe that such developments can be reversed. There are those who believe that their community still has the key to the proper interpretation of scripture, whether this be in the form of some infallible teaching office, of some

Box 5

The Protestant principle that everyone could be his or her own interpreter of scripture (as opposed to the Catholic view that the tradition of the Church as established in the church councils was the true interpreter of scripture) was pilloried by a 16th-century Catholic scholar in the following terms:

> This Biblicist is a single person. The fathers of the council can be any number. This Biblicist is a sheep...the fathers of the council are pastors and bishops. This Biblicist prays by himself. The fathers of the council pray for all who are present at the council, indeed for the whole Christian world...This Biblicist may be an uneducated woman. They...are the most learned men in the Christian world.
>
> Valerianus Magni, *De acatholicorum credendi regular indicium* (An assessment of the rule of believing of non-Catholics).

theological rule or confession which can act as a test of true readings of the texts, or indeed of a historical method which can deliver the original, single meaning of the text.

The difficulty with theological keys is this: either they are so specific, so closely tied to one particular community, that they are of little use in resolving disputes between communities, or they are so general, framed so widely, that they fail to address points of specific difference. If, for example, a particular church wishes to uphold one of the Reformation confessions of faith as its 'subordinate standard of faith', this may indeed enable it to adjudicate in internal disputes about the proper interpretation of scripture: it will not, however, enable the resolution of interdenominational differences, where it is precisely the difference between the various confessions of faith which is at issue. If, on the other hand, one were to propose some much more general principle of interpretation, say that all interpretations should be broadly Trinitarian in scope, this would generate only a relatively weak set of rules whereby to adjudicate between different Christian interpretations. It would of course also be too specifically Christian to be of use in cases of interfaith disagreement.

The alternative to such an approach is to try to find some apparently neutral method of interpretation to which all can appeal, regardless of cultural stance. Here the historical critical method has seemed to many to be a most promising candidate. Just as Luther asked 'what the Apostle wanted' as a way to resolve disputes over the meaning of a text in Romans, so one might seek to resolve other disputes by searching for the original meaning intended by the author. There are a number of problems with this proposal. In the first place, it is doubtful whether authorial intention will do the job that it is asked to. Are authors' intentions as clear as all that? T. S. Eliot once replied when asked if an interpretation of his poetry corresponded to what he had meant: 'What I meant is what I wrote.' Secondly, and perhaps more problematically, historians are inevitably influenced by their own point of view. This is partly a matter of their place within a particular tradition of reading, with its own body of knowledge, cultural beliefs, and standpoints, and partly a matter of their own tastes, preferences, and prejudices, formed in a broader cultural context. All of this will shape their judgements, with the result that historians will inevitably produce a plurality of readings. One would have to be blind as a historian to the diversity of historical readings (produced by eminent scholars) not to realize the truth of this. It does not mean that appeal to historical arguments may never be of use; nor does it mean that we learn nothing about the texts from such enquiries. It does mean that we will be most unlikely to resolve many disputes by recourse to such a line of argument.

So perhaps readers of the Bible will have to live with the fact that it has a rich potential for generating different meanings. Maybe, indeed, they should come to see this not simply as a problem with the Bible, but also as part of its very strength. This has serious consequences. It means first that the normative function of the Bible for any community is significantly weakened. If the Bible is recognized as essentially capable of many meanings, its use as a code of conduct or indeed as a rule of faith will be limited. But has this not always been the case? The fact that Jews will appeal to the Talmudim for rulings on matters of practice and belief and that Christians have appealed to some rule of faith or to the canons of the ecumenical councils to regulate their affairs suggests clearly enough that in practice it has always been accepted that the Bible was either too rich or too diverse or too ambiguous to do the job of a Code Napoléon.

On the other hand, recognizing the Bible's potential for generating different meanings does not mean that its formative function is weakened in the same way. The whole point of our argument has been to show how powerful the influence of the Bible has been in the formation of a whole range of communities. Such power is not without its dangers. It has generated some deeply oppressive settler communities, just as it has produced reformers, liberationist politicians, and peacemakers.

What it certainly means is that we have to learn to read the Bible more critically. We have to become better attuned to the different voices within the biblical texts. Equally we also need to be aware of the different kinds of uses to which the Bible may be put and to learn to discriminate among them.

In these tasks the various approaches that we have considered all have their role to play. The historian of religion precisely by discerning different tendencies and influences in the texts may help us to be more aware of their complexity. Schüssler-Fiorenza's analysis of the patriarchal tendencies in Luke alerts us to how certain traditions have been marginalized in the Bible—and indeed in subsequent readings of the Bible—in ways which enable us to hear voices which we might otherwise have missed. Similarly, Mary Grey's imaginative use of wilderness motifs may serve to inspire people to live through the toils of a church emerging from patriarchy and to discover forms of communal living which are more integrative, more humane.

Again, readers will be guided by the rules and interpretative practices of the communities to which they belong. Those within Christian communities will be deeply influenced by the form(s) of the Christian canon. Its setting of the New Testament alongside the Old creates, as we saw in Desmond Tutu's reading of the Naboth story, a powerful theological framework within which to read the texts.

Even so, readers will have to judge for themselves between the different interpretations which any such approach makes possible. In this they will in a sense be thrown back on their own moral resources. But it is not simply a matter of individuals sitting in judgement over the biblical texts: the process of reading is more complex. In the first place, readers are rarely alone: they belong to communities which have been shaped by the text and which have in turn schooled their own moral senses. Thus the thoughtful reader is always engaged in a process of testing inherited moral senses against the texts and, as we have seen in so many cases, against their own experience. Will it stretch or will it break? Are there other senses among the readings which are possible from a particular perspective which will lead out of seeming impasses, which can bring renewal to traditions which are drying up or, worse, leading to oppression and self-deception?

Moreover, in this process readers are not simply dependent upon their own inherited values. As they learn to discriminate between the different voices in the texts, between different readings and constructions of the text, their moral and religious imagination and judgement is informed and sharpened. Where such discriminating and attentive reading occurs, communal traditions will be nourished and kept alive; where they are absent or marginalized, the tradition will wither. Even then, not all may be lost: from time to time there emerge moral and prophetic figures in whom the ideas and images of the texts have taken deep root, who may renew their inherited traditions or else generate new communities of their own.

One of the remarkable features of the Bible which we have noticed too little is its age. Its earliest material is some 3,000 years old; most of it is 2,000 years old and the New Testament only just slightly younger. From time to time people cast doubt on the ability of such ancient texts to speak to people so far removed in time. Certainly if the texts were limited only to the meaning which they carried (and were intended to carry) for their first hearers, we might well wonder whether they would have any future in an age so different as ours. But their history demonstrates that their stories, images, metaphors, and moral and religious concepts have shaped and continue to shape the experience and understanding of peoples of great diversity. Recent history in Africa and Asia suggests that there is no diminishing of this power. What are required are discriminating readers, alert to its life-giving potential, on their guard against its darker tones.

References and further reading

Unless stated otherwise in the text, biblical references are taken from the Revised Standard Version.

Chapter 1: The Bible in the modern world: classic or sacred text?

Daniel Boyarin, *A Radical Jew: Paul and the Politics of Identity* (University of California Press, Berkeley, 1994).

Malise Ruthven, *The Divine Supermarket: Shopping for God in America* (Vintage, London, 1991).

Chapter 2: How the biblical books were written

A good introduction to the history of the formation of the books of the Bible is to be found in the relevant articles in the new *Anchor Bible Dictionary* (Doubleday, New York, 1992). The article on Torah (Pentateuch), vol. 6, pp. 605–22, by Richard Friedman is particularly helpful. For the Synoptic Gospels, see Scot McKnight, John K. Riches, William Telford, and Christopher M. Tuckett, *Synoptic Gospels* (Bloomsbury, London, 2001); Graham Stanton, *The Gospels and Jesus* (Oxford University Press, Oxford, 1989). For a general introduction to Paul and his writings, see E. P. Sanders, *Paul* (Oxford University Press, Oxford, 1991). John Barton's *A History of the Bible: The Book and its Faiths* (Penguin Books, London, 2020) makes the point about Hebrew narrative styles and the closeness of saga styles to oral materials. His book is a rich source of insight into the historical processes which produced the Bible.

Chapter 3: The making of the Bible

The articles on 'Canon' by James A. Sanders and Harry Y. Gamble in the *Anchor Bible Dictionary*, vol. 1, pp. 837–61, are very useful. John Barton has made a particular study of the origin of the canon and of the nature of its authority: see especially his *People of the Book? The Authority of the Bible in Christianity* (SPCK, London, 1988); and *Making the Christian Bible* (Darton, Longman and Todd, London, 1997). See too James A. Sanders, *From Sacred Story to Sacred Text* (Fortress Press, Philadelphia, 1987). Moshe Halberthal, *People of the Book: Canon, Meaning, and Authority* (Harvard University Press, Cambridge, Mass., 1997), provides a fascinating discussion of different kinds of canonical authority and the effect canonization has on the way texts are read.

Chapter 4: Translation, production, and distribution of the Bible

This chapter owes a great deal to the following contributions to John Riches (ed.), *The New Cambridge History of the Bible: From 1750 to the Present* (Cambridge University Press, Cambridge, 2015): Leslie Howsam and Scott Mclaren, 'Producing the text: production and distribution of popular editions of the Bible', pp. 49–82; Lamin Sanneh, 'Translations of the Bible and the cultural impulse', pp. 83–123; Néstor Míguez, 'The Bible in Latin America', pp. 427–60; David Thompson, 'The Bible in Europe', pp. 497–519. There is also much to be learnt from Diarmaid MacCulloch's *Reformation: Europe's House Divided 1490–1700* (Penguin, London, 2004); see p. 75 for an important reminder of lay interest in the reading of the Bible before Luther. Lamin Sanneh's views are developed more fully in his *Translating the Messsage: The Missionary Impact on Culture* (Orbis Books, Maryknoll, NY, 1997), quotation p. 160.

Chapter 5: Jewish and Christian readings of the Binding of Isaac

The text of the book of Jubilees is to be found in J. Charlesworth (ed.), *The Old Testament Pseudepigrapha* (Darton, Longman and Todd, London, 1985), vol. 2, pp. 35–142; Philo's *De Abrahamo* is in the

Loeb Classical Library Philo vol. 6 (Harvard University Press, Cambridge, Mass., 1984), pp. 2–135. Shalom Spiegel, *The Last Trial: On the Legends and Lore of the Command to Abraham to offer Isaac as a Sacrifice: The Akedah* (Jewish Lights Publishing, Woodstock, Vt, 1993), provides a rich discussion of Jewish retellings of the story, together with the text of the poems cited here: pp. 20–1; 148–9. The quotation from Judah Goldin's introduction is taken from p. xx. Søren Kierkegaard's discussion is in *Fear and Trembling* (ed. and trans. H. V. and E. H. Hong, Princeton University Press, Princeton, 1983, quotation, p. 21).

Chapter 6: Galatians through history

This chapter draws largely on my *Galatians Through the Centuries*, Wiley-Blackwell Biblical Commentaries (Wiley-Blackwell, Chichester, 2008).

For the text of works cited: Marcion's works have been lost and need to be reconstructed: see Judith M. Lieu, *Marcion and the Making of a Heretic: God and Scripture in the Second Century* (Cambridge University Press, Cambridge, 2015). The Gospel of Philip is found in Bentley Layton, *The Gnostic Scriptures*, Anchor Bible Reference Library (Yale University Press, New Haven, 2007). There is an excellent edition of Augustine's commentary in Eric Plumer, *Augustine's Commentary on Galatians: Introduction, Text, Translation, and Notes* (Oxford University Press, Oxford, 2003). The most accessible edition of John Chrysostom's commentary is in the Library of the Nicene and Post-Nicene Fathers (NPNF), vol 13. For Aquinas, see his *Commentary on St. Paul's Epistle to the Galatians*, trans. F. R. Larcher, OP, Aquinas Scripture Series (Magi Books, Albany, NY, 1966). Luther's Galatians Commentary is found in *Luther's Works: American Edition*, vol. 27, ed. Jaroslav Pelikan (Concordia Publishing House, St Louis, 1973) (LW). I have quoted from the English translation which Bunyan and the Wesleys will have read: *A Commentary on St. Paul's Epistle to the Galatians. Based on Lectures Delivered by Martin Luther at the University of* Wittenberg in the Year 1531 and first published in 1535. A Revised and Completed Translation Based on the 'Middleton' Edition of the English Version of 1575 (James Clarke, London, 1953), pp. 500–1. The quotations about the Wesleys are taken from the Preface, pp. 1–15 by the editor, Philip S. Watson. For Calvin see John Calvin,

The Institutes of the Christian Religion (James Clarke, London, 1949) (*Inst.*). For Bunyan, see John Bunyan, *Grace Abounding to the Chief of Sinners*, ed. John Brown (Cambridge University Press, Cambridge, 1907), p. 41.

The question, was Paul responsible for the development of the introspective consciousness of the West, was raised by Krister Stendahl in an address to the Annual Meeting of the American Psychological Society in 1961: 'The Apostle Paul and the introspective conscience of the West', in *Paul Among Jews and Gentiles and other Essays* (Fortress Press, Philadelphia, 1976). New Testament scholars have, for the most part, followed Stendahl in attributing this development to Augustine and Luther, and in seeing it in wholly negative terms: 'The introspective conscience is a Western development and a Western plague' (p. 17). For a critical response, see my 'Readings of Augustine on Paul: their impact on critical studies of Paul' in Daniel Patte and Eugene TeSelle (eds), *Engaging Augustine on Romans: Self, Context, and Theology in Interpretation* (Trinity Press International, Harrisburg, Pa, 2002), pp. 173–98. For a weighty counterview of the origins and nature of Western inwardness, as leading to the affirmation of ordinary life, see Charles Taylor, *Sources of the Self: The Making of Modern Identity* (Cambridge University Press, Cambridge, 1989).

Chapter 7: The Bible and its critics

For Luther on the gift of righteousness: John Dillenberger, *Martin Luther: Selections from his Writings* (Doubleday, New York, 1961), p. 11. For Melanchthon's rejection of Copernicus: Klaus Scholder, *The Birth of Modern Critical Theology: Origins and Problems of Biblical Criticism in the Seventeenth Century* (SCM Press, London, 1990), p. 49, citing *Corpus Reformatorum* 13, cols 216–17. For the view that knowledge of the true causes of the movements of heavenly bodies is beyond the reach of our minds: Scholder, *The Birth of Modern Critical Theology*, pp. 47–8. For Thomas Sherlock: Leslie Stephen, *History of English Thought in the Eighteenth Century* (Rupert Hart-Davis, London, 1962), 2 vols, vol. 1, pp. 203–4. Quite the best treatment of the rise of biblical criticism is to be found in Scholder's *The Birth of Modern Critical Theology*. Dillenberger's *Martin Luther: Selections from his Writings* gives a useful selection. Luther's discussion of his attempts to understand Romans 1:17 is to be found in The Preface to the Latin Writings of 1545. Stephen's *History of English Thought in the Eighteenth Century* is a classic treatment of English Deism. Reimarus: *Fragments*, ed. C. H. Talbert (SCM Press, London, 1970), gives a translation of only some of the sections of Reimarus' Apology which Lessing published. Henry Chadwick (ed.), *Lessing's Theological Writings: Selections in Translation* (A & C Black, London, 1956), gives some of the other important Lessing texts. Albert Schweitzer, *The Quest for the Historical Jesus: A Critical Study of its Progress from Reimarus to Wrede* (A & C Black, London, 1910, 2nd edn. 1936), is the most lasting literary work of this theologian, musicologist, organist, missionary doctor, and philosopher of religion.

Chapter 8: The Bible in the post-colonial world

An excellent guide to the use of the Bible in the colonial period is provided by Michael Prior, CM, *The Bible and Colonialism: A Moral Critique* (Sheffield Academic Press, Sheffield, 1997. I have quoted from the following works cited by Prior: Pablo Richard, '1492: The violence of God and the future of Christianity', in Leonardo Boff and Virgil Elizondo (eds), '1492–1992: The Voice of the Victims', *Concilium*, 1990 (SCM Press, London, 1990), pp. 59–67 for the open letter from various indigenous groups inviting the Pope to take back the Bible to Europe; Maximiliano Salinas, 'The voices of those who speak up for the victims', *Concilium*, 1990 (SCM Press, London, 1990), pp. 101–9, for Bartolomé de Las Casas' sermon at Pentecost in 1514. The Fray Toribio quotation, is found in Prior, *The Bible and Colonialism*, p. 61.

Gustavo Gutiérrez, A Theology of Liberation (SCM Press, London, 1971) is one of the classics of Liberation Theology. His later *The God of Life* (SCM Press, London, 1991) is in the form of a biblical meditation. G. Pixley, *On Exodus: A Liberation Perspective* (Orbis, Maryknoll, NY, 1983) takes up the work of Norman Gottwald, Israel, 1250–1050 BCE *The Tribes of Yahweh: A Sociology of Religion of Liberated* (SCM Press, London, 1979). Desmond Tutu, *Hope and Suffering* (Collins, London, 1984), brings together a collection of Tutu's sermons and speeches delivered during the apartheid era. Musa W. Dube, 'Readings of Semoya: Botswana women's interpretation of Matt. 15: 21–8', in Gerald West and Musa W. Dube (eds), *'Reading With': An Exploration of the Interface between Critical and Ordinary Readings of the Bible: African Overtures*, Semeia 73 (Scholars Press, Atlanta, Ga, 1996), is part of a volume of essays exploring African readings of the Bible.

Chapter 9: The Bible in politics

Quotations from Luther are taken from John Dillenberger, *Martin Luther: Selections from his Writings* (Doubleday, New York, 1961). Ulrich Luz, 'Die Bergpredigt im Spiegel ihrer Wirkungsgeschichte', in Jürgen Moltmann (ed.), *Nachfolge und Bergpredigt* (Kaiser Verlag, Munich, 1981), pp. 31–72. Daniel J. Boorstin, *The Americans: The Colonial Experience* (Vintage Books, New York, 1958), pp. 33–69, gives a critical view of Quaker history in Pennsylvania. The classic Quaker text is to be found in Rufus M. Jones (ed.), *The Journal of George Fox* (Friends United Press, Richmond, Ind., 1976). Phyllis Tribble's *Texts of Terror: Literary Feminist Readings of the Biblical Narratives*, Overtures to Biblical Theology (Fortress Press, Philadelphia, 1984) exposes the dark and deep roots of patriarchy in the biblical texts. Elisabeth Schüssler-Fiorenza, *In Memory of Her: A Feminist Theological Reconstruction of Christian Origins* (Crossroad, New York, 1983), uses historical research into the New Testament to uncover the more liberative strands which lie behind it. The importance of this for the understanding of the Church is drawn out in her *Discipleship of Equals: A Critical Feminist Ekklesia-logy of Liberation* (SCM Press, London, 1993). Mary Grey, *Beyond the Dark Night: A Way Forward for the Church* (Cassell, London, 1997), looks for ways out of the present dilemma of the Catholic Church.

Chapter 10: The Bible in high and popular culture

Northrop Frye, *The Great Code: The Bible and Literature* (Harcourt Brace Jovanovich, New York, 1981), was one of the foundational works in the study of the influence of the Bible on European literature. For a general introduction to Bach's music, see Malcolm Boyd, *Bach* (Oxford University Press, Oxford, 1990). Owen's poems are most easily available in C. Day Lewis (ed.), *The Collected*

Poems of Wilfred Owen (Chatto & Windus, London, 1977). Mieke Bal, *Reading 'Rembrandt': Beyond the Word–Image Opposition* (Cambridge University Press, Cambridge, 1992), gives a fascinating account of Rembrandt as an interpreter of the Bible. Peter Black with Erma Hermens provided a wonderfully detailed study of the Glasgow *Entombment Sketch* in *Rembrandt and the Passion* (Prestel, London, 2012). Margaret Atwood, *The Handmaid's Tale* (Virago Press, London, 1987) is also discussed in David Jasper and Stephen Prickett (eds), *The Bible and Literature: A Reader* (Blackwell, Oxford, 1999). Its sequel was published as *The Testaments* (Chatto & Windus, London, 2019).

Chapter 11: Conclusion

Robert Morgan with John Barton, *Biblical Interpretation* (Oxford University Press, Oxford, 1988). Valerianus Magni is quoted from Klaus Scholder, *The Birth of Modern Critical Theology: Origins and Problems of Biblical Criticism in the Seventeenth Century* (SCM Press, London, 1990), p. 18.

Index of biblical references

For the benefit of digital users, indexed terms that span two pages (e.g., 52–53) may, on occasion, appear on only one of those pages.

General index

For the benefit of digital users, indexed terms that span two pages (e.g., 52–53) may, on occasion, appear on only one of those pages.

A

B

C

D

E

F

G

H

I

J

K

L

M

N

O

P

Q

R

S

T

W

Y

BIBLICAL ARCHAEOLOGY

A Very Short Introduction

Eric H. Cline

Archaeologist Eric H. Cline here offers a complete overview of this exciting field. He discusses the early pioneers, the origins of biblical archaeology as a discipline, and the major controversies that first prompted explorers to go in search of sites that would "prove" the Bible. He then surveys some of the most well-known modern archaeologists, the sites that are essential sources of knowledge for biblical archaeology, and some of the most important discoveries that have been made in the last half century, including the Dead Sea Scrolls and the Tel Dan Stele.

www.oup.com/vsi

THE REFORMATION

A Very Short Introduction

Peter Marshall

The Reformation transformed Europe, and left an indelible mark on the modern world. It began as an argument about what Christians needed to do to be saved, but rapidly engulfed society in a series of fundamental changes. This *Very Short Introduction* provides a lively and up-to-date guide to the process. Peter Marshall argues that the Reformation was not a solely European phenomenon, but that varieties of faith exported from Europe transformed Christianity into a truly world religion. It explains doctrinal debates in a clear and non-technical way, but is equally concerned to demonstrate the effects the Reformation had on politics, society, art, and minorities.

www.oup.com/vsi

THE NEW TESTAMENT

A Very Short Introduction

Luke Timothy Johnson

As part of the Christian Bible, the New Testament is at once widely influential and increasingly unknown. Those who want to know the basics can find in this introduction the sort of information that locates these ancient writings in their historical and literary context. In addition to providing the broad conceptual and factual framework for the New Testament — including the process by which distinct compositions became a sacred book — this introduction provides as well a more detailed examination of specific compositions that have had particularly strong influence, including Paul's letters to the Corinthians and Romans, the four Gospels, and the Book of Revelation.

www.oup.com/vsi